Gardening for the Vase

OWEN A REID

Gardening for the Vase

Flower Arrangements by Joan Oosthuizen
Photographs by John Brunda

Jonathan Ball Publishers
Johannesburg

Human & Rousseau
Cape Town and Pretoria

To my darling wife, Gwyn, whose love and
encouragement make all things possible.

First published in 1987 by
Jonathan Ball Publishers
P O Box 548
Bergvlei
2012 Johannesburg
and
Human & Rousseau (Pty) Ltd
State House, 3 – 9 Rose Street
Cape Town
and Atrium Building, 60 Glenwood Road
Pretoria

ISBN 0 86850 109 3

Cover design by Etienne van Duyker
Design and phototypesetting by
Book Productions, Pretoria
Colour reproduction by Lithotechnik, Pretoria
Printed and bound by National Book Printers,
Goodwood, Cape

Contents

Acknowledgements

This book was made possible with the help of innumerable gardening friends, who not only allowed me to take photographs in their gardens but also offered much helpful advice. They are far too many to mention but their assistance is nonetheless greatly appreciated.

Special people to whom I am particularly grateful include: my wonderful partners in preparing this book – Joan Oosthuizen, who not only provided many ideas and much advice but who so lovingly created her beautiful floral arrangements for perfectionist John Brunda to photograph; to my friend and partner Keith Kirsten for editing and checking all horticultural facts, and to Margot Murray who so untiringly and meticulously read and re-read my manuscript and made valuable corrections and suggestions.

A special word of thanks to Emily Sengati, who not only helped Joan greatly in preparing material for use in vase photographs but also cleared and tidied up at the end of photographic sessions and in between provided innumerable cups of tea to cheer the weary.

Special thanks to my wonderful staff at Waterkloof Garden Centre, who were so helpful in many ways; Mrs Danielle Crafford and the members of the Pretoria Chapter of Ikebana International; Mrs Marjorie McLeod, whose beautiful Florida bulb garden is opened to the public each spring to raise funds for charity; Mrs J R Flynn, whose beautiful garden provided the setting for many pictures and Mr Floris Barnhoorn of Hadeco Bulb Company for providing bulb charts and a number of bulb pictures.

Introduction

Garden-grown flowers are one of the great pleasures of life – a delight in the border and a bonus when arranged to brighten interiors. Plan your garden for picking and you will gain twice the pleasure from your efforts.

Nature is so prolific that we have many thousands of plants from which to choose when designing our gardens. All plant types, whether they are shrubs, trees, climbers, annuals, perennials or ground covers, include varieties which produce material suitable for picking, so why not choose those which have a dual purpose, garden and vase?

Planting with the vase in mind doubles your blessings: the more material you acquire for picking, the more varied and attractive your garden becomes, while the more you plant, the greater is your choice of flower and foliage when gathering for your arrangements.

Obviously you will want not only colourful flowers but shrubs and trees to provide foliage of contrasting colours, as well as plants of varying texture, from light and feathery grasses to trees with large, leathery leaves, all of which will add interest to your border.

This book has been written to show those gardeners who believe that borders, rather than vases, are for flowers, that with a little planning it is possible to have a show garden and a picking garden at the same time.

There was a time when many gardeners merely grew flowers for the house, without worrying too much about what the garden looked like, as long as it was colourful. Then, swinging full circle, there followed a mania for low-maintenance gardens which cut out practically all annuals and relied on shrubs and perennials for colour. The garden for the vase is the middle road – why should you not combine the two types?

For the flower arranger the colour garden has great attraction, but oddly enough the low-maintenance garden has more to offer. While flowers are used to complement the greenery, the emphasis shifts to more diverse plantings: an abundance of foliage of varying colour, shape and size, interesting berried branches, blossoms, plumes and blooms, flowers, shrubs, trees and climbers. All these features contribute to an attractive garden and in their turn provide exciting material for indoor display.

The germ of the idea which produced this book dates back to the late 1960s. As a proud new homeowner I began to take an interest in gardening, but was shocked to discover that every time I produced anything in the garden of which I was proud, it would soon disappear, only to reappear later in a vase.

Outrage and alarm stalked the corridors of our home for several seasons. My delight of the morning at seeing a delicate 'Peace' rose blooming at my front door would turn to despair in the evening when, on returning home, I would find my pride and joy adorning the hallway.

The disappearance of a rose here and a gardenia there was trauma enough, but when I found practically a whole bed of sparkling nasturtiums 'transported' to the lounge, with some of them even appearing in my salad, I knew I was beaten and surrendered myself to the idea of a garden for the vase.

My first reaction was to produce a garden with the appearance of a commercial venture: flowers growing in serried ranks, all ready for the knife. Mercifully, sanity prevailed and I realised that by planting a garden rather in the way one produces a flower arrangement, with focal point, and a tasteful combination of colour, contrast and texture, it was possible to please everyone – to provide for the visual enjoyment of family and friends, whilst also supplying cutting flowers and foliage for twelve months of the year.

The purpose of this book then is twofold:
• To offer suggestions on how to go about planning your garden for the vase, and
• how to use that material in as simple, yet as attractive a manner as possible.

Landscaping an arranger's garden is really no different from landscaping any other garden, the principles of design remain the same. It is only in the planting that there is a difference in emphasis.

If your garden is already established, some re-arrangement may be necessary.

With just a bunch of cornflowers it is possible to add charm to your home without any lessons in flower arranging.

viii

A few calendulas placed in a dumpy vase by a busy housewife add character to this farm kitchen.

You will need to examine carefully what is useful and worth retaining. With a new garden you have no problems, and can plant only what you want and need.

There are many reasons for planning your garden but two important considerations are financial. The well thought-out and well-designed garden will save expensive mistakes in over-buying or buying the wrong plants and, secondly, will enable you to have plants both useful in the border and suitable for picking. With the cost of cut flowers today, a garden filled with suitable material for indoor decoration can save you a fortune. Having to buy flowers limits your ability to arrange; a garden allows you to give free rein to individual imagination and flair.

Although economy may play an important role in growing your own material, the major reason must remain pleasure. There are few activities as tranquil and pleasant as wandering through a garden in the cool of the day – be it early morning or late afternoon – picking flowers for the vase.

With the huge number of indigenous plants and suitable conditions for the growing of so many exotic flowers in our wonderful South African climate, flower arrangers here are more blessed than those in

practically any other country in the world. In most parts of the Republic it is certainly possible to have both material and colour in the garden for 365 days of the year.

Although a book about growing plants for use in arrangements, *Gardening for the Vase* is also intended to show the reader that you don't have to be an expert arranger to enjoy flowers in the home. My aim is to encourage you to be creative and to use the material you have at hand. Professionally styled arrangements have their place, but a posy of violets at a breakfast table or a few blossoms floating in a bowl can be equally charming.

This is not a book for professional gardeners and flower arranging experts, but I hope that they too may find something of interest. It is rather for those busy people who have no time to join clubs and classes to learn how to arrange expertly.

My hope is that it will enable you to enjoy your garden and at the same time enliven your home with the least amount of work, in the shortest possible time and at minimal cost.

I have enjoyed the valuable assistance of an extremely talented gardener with a vast amount of experience both in growing and in flower arranging, an artist with both brush and blooms – Mrs Joan Oosthuizen.

Joan prepared most of the arrangements in this book, for photographing by John Brunda, using only a few flowers or concentrating on one variety, in order to show that it is possible to produce exciting displays which are both simple and practical. She believes a few well-chosen blooms can be as striking as a multitude and her work in this book proves the point. Further she has shown by use of foliage that it is possible to have displays with colour and contrast even when there is not a single flower in the garden.

A feature of her work has been her use of varieties of flowers that are not normally thought of as flower arranging material – such as plumbago and petunias. She has also chosen to use types of flowers which are often seen growing on flat balconies and window-boxes or in townhouse gardens – such as daisies, nasturtiums and geraniums.

A chapter of the book has been devoted to

extending the life of cut flowers, to avoid stripping the garden. Many plants can also be preserved and kept for a long time, even years, such as the leaves of loquat, magnolia and the dainty pittosporum, as well as hydrangea and protea heads, and the frothy mini-flowers of *Statice latifolia* and gypsophila. These may be used over and over again for years. Long life in the vase is important. Consider the number of plants you will save from cutting if you can lengthen the life of picked flowers by even 10 per cent.

Here also Joan Oosthuizen has helped me in experimenting to find the most successful ways of preserving certain flowers and checking on the lasting quality of many varieties.

The term 'vase' as it is used in the title of this book means a flower holder in the very broadest sense: I refer to a table-napkin on a dinner table, with an hibiscus flower resting on it: a huge container suitable for a vast church arrangement or a salad in which flowers provide both food and decoration.

To facilitate gardening for the vase, plants are suggested for practically every purpose and situation. Not only do they provide colour and texture, contrast and variety – there are plants for screening, plants for rockeries, even plants for cold gardens and shade gardens.

A great many lists are provided, including one for fragrance both in the garden and indoors; it is most agreeable to have sweet-smelling flowers and foliage in the home, particularly for scenting the loo rather than using aerosol ersatz.

Growing cutting plants for large gardens is easy but with small and townhouse-type gardens the range is limited, and so here too I have provided lists of suitable flowers and foliage.

Flowers have a wonderful way of saying 'Welcome' – be they in the garden or the vase. Let's go gardening!

Owen A Reid

I *Your grand design*

Designing a garden for the vase may become a love of a lifetime, an on-going programme which never really ends, as you find more and more interesting material with which to fill your garden. Do not, however, let your love smother your original plan – never grow just for the sake of growing, casting the principles of good landscaping to the wind.

Landscaping is of vital importance in any garden, whatever the size or nature of the plot. Be it a barren erf or a lush overgrown jungle there must be a plan, no matter how simple.

Remember that a garden is for outdoor living and should give pleasure to the whole family. You may well design it with your major objective being material for the vase, but never let this dominate your planning to the exclusion of all else.

Footballs, galloping cowboys and Red Indians, as well as dogs, have an unfortunate habit of damaging things and it is up to you to provide areas where children may have ample space for a cricket game, without topping the daisies, and an area for the family dog to bury bones without digging up the dahlias. If not, life for the family may become a nightmare.

While landscaping is what makes a garden liveable, it is unneccesary to go to the expense of engaging a landscape architect or designer. You can plan your own garden very adequately, simply by giving the matter some thought.

Always remember that the intention of landscaping is to maximize the comfort and pleasure of a garden. A purely utilitarian plot, with plants grown just for picking would be an uninspiring prospect.

The principles of landscaping are universal, whether you are designing a low maintenance garden, an indigenous one, a bower of colour or a garden for the vase. The only difference is that of emphasis. These principles apply whether you live in the plush suburbs of Constantia and Houghton or own a beach front plot at Umbogintwini.

To begin, decide at the outset what the main purpose of your garden is to be and remember that it is possible to plan a garden with more than one objective in view. It could, for instance, be designed as a very formal garden, yet still provide picking material, or it could be a very informal one, filled with tropical plants and planned for entertaining.

What is important is to decide on a plan of action at the beginning and then *stick* to it. Gardens are never static, they are always changing, but it is very difficult to alter your course drastically – such as turning a basically formal design with straight lines and angles, hedges and fences, into a natural one with flowing contours and rough textures. Cosmetic changes may always be made but try not to alter basic design as you go along or you will end up with a hodge-podge. It is not necessary to put the whole of your grand design into operation in one fell swoop but you must be able to see how you are going to progress step by step.

With your grand plan it is important to lay the foundation for good indoor-outdoor relationships by ensuring that living areas are a convenient extension of the house. Try, for instance, to arrange for your braai area to be near the kitchen for easy serving; situate the play area within view of mother's sewing-room but away from where father takes his afternoon nap; and don't forget to consider the neighbours.

Although your garden, planned as it is for its picking material, will eventually differ greatly from most other gardens, in that it will to a certain extent become a collector's garden, it will need to be made habitable before the major plantings of your favourite flowers and foliage can take place.

The problems in garden layout are in fact much the same as those faced when decorating the interior of the house. You will need to consider such features as your entrance (hallway), driveway (passages), garden furniture and braai equipment (household fittings), screening fences and hedges (walls and partitions) and even the circulation of air and windbreaks (air-conditioning).

When visualizing your plot, whether it be a garden you are starting from scratch or a re-modelling job, you should first take an inventory. Assess what you have in the way of trees, mounds, hollows, rocky outcrops, pleasant views, strong winds, unsightly neighbouring buildings and similar considerations. Always look carefully to see what is worth saving, particularly if you are re-designing an established erf. Make the most of what you inherit when taking over a ready-made garden. An old tree might at first appear a problem, but with a little thought and planning you could transform it into a feature.

When planning consider such items as:
- screens and climate control
- boundaries
- vistas and views
- service areas
- play areas (pool, tennis court, sauna, jacuzzi)
- entertainment area
- entrance and driveway
- patios
- flooring (lawns, paved areas and pathways)
- water features
- special features (bird baths, statues and containers, gazebo, herb garden and rockery).

There are many other things you might like to include, such as a private hideaway for nude sunbathing, a sauna perhaps or even a croquet lawn.

It is wise to make a list of all such things, giving particular consideration to your special interests – floral material for the vase. In addition to the placing of plants for picking wherever you can, you might also like to have a special cutting garden – an area for growing quantities of flowers such as sweet peas and dahlias, or some other favourites, in convenient proximity to your work area but away from the public view.

Always remember that those beautiful landscapes you admire in other people's gardens don't just happen – they are planned. This is the key to any successful project. Time spent on planning will repay you many times over.

Be your garden ever so small, you will be surprised at just what you can include with proper forethought. Think big when plan-

Statues make fine focal points in areas consisting mainly of shrubs or trees.

ning. Aim at including all the many projects you wish to have in your scheme. But a word of warning – getting in all your projects does not mean you can allow yourself to over-plant. When planting always consider the eventual size of the plant – don't be deceived by its appearance at time of planting.

The wise gardener will also not fight conditions prevailing on his plot. If it's a frosty garden, don't go tropical; don't try to level a sloping property – design the garden in keeping with the site.

With your initial plan always be totally ruthless in removing features you don't want. If you fail in this they will always irritate you and when later you do decide to remove whatever it is that troubles you the cost will probably be double. What is more, it will probably upset the surrounding plantings. Even transplant or remove plants if they are in the wrong place.

Put your plan on paper. This method proves successful for most people and it is certainly the one used by professional landscapers. First indicate on the schematic drawing of your plot, the position and shape of your house, as well as prominent physical features such as a washline, a summer house, a large hollow or mound.

Although trained men may visualize finished plans on rough pieces of paper, it is a good idea for the amateur to make his or her drawing on graph paper – using a 10 mm to a metre scale. And don't think you can do without a plan. There are far too many aspects which you must consider for you to be able to successfully carry them about in your head, especially as you will be chopping and changing a great deal initially until the puzzle falls into place.

Once the permanent features have been drawn in, move on to the broad outline of what you need. It is a good idea to consider

Even a play area, such as a swimming pool surround, may be used for beds of cutting material, as long as they don't interfere with the main purpose of the facility.

your perimeters first. Use a piece of tracing paper over your plan until you have decided firmly where certain features are to go.

There will certainly be sections along your borders where screening will be necessary, either to block out an unpleasant view of the neighbour's property or their view of yours, or even to block the view of passersby. Screening may also be used to block off cold winds or to cut out some of the noise of passing traffic. It is as well to decide at this point whether you want to use a wall, stout fencing or plants for the job.

You should also consider how to frame a view from your property which you enjoy. It is a good idea to draw at the edge of your plan any attractive features beyond your

2

Screening is one of the most important features in any garden and here plants have been used cleverly to hide an ugly swimming pool fence and provide material for the vase.

borders – be they near or distant. In this way you can blot out ugly views while retaining the good ones for 'inclusion' in your garden. There may be a fine view of distant hills, or your neighbour's magnificent oak, or a spectacularly colourful maple – you may even wish to include the curl of a charming chimney. By this method it is possible to give your garden a far more spacious feel and you are cleverly expanding your borders.

If there is no view beyond your garden walls, try to create one within your boundaries. There are many ways in which this can be done, but a favourite is to create a tunnel view with a statue, gazebo or just a bench under a tree at the end of it. Try using strik-ing plants such as a group of silver birches for focal points, thus drawing the eye to a specific section of the garden. Of course, special features such as ponds, fountains or waterfalls may also be used when creating a view.

Once your borders and views are sorted out, it is time to draw in those other major features: the vegetable patch and compost heap – both of which must be in a sunny spot, not in one of those narrow areas between buildings; a play area; swimming pool; deck or patio. At the same time examine carefully the positioning of an item such as a summer house in relation to your view. See that you have no deciduous trees near the pool, and ensure that the trees will not block out the view so carefully framed when preparing your border. Remember that the tennis court should lie from north to south. This sounds very elementary but it is aston-ishing how often mistakes of this type are made and realized too late, involving great expense and trouble to rectify.

Although no plan is final, do try to make firm and carefully considered decisions on major items and expensive features. Cos-metic changes may be done at any time, but to discover that your pool or tennis court has been badly placed may be disastrous.

II *Where to start*

Faced with a bare erf and a plan, many new gardeners have the problem of 'where to start?' – and of course there is no fixed point for turning the first sod, it is all a matter of what is important to you.

A good idea, however, is to start with the basic necessities – such as erecting the washline, placing the dog's kennel and positioning the children's sand pit.

Certainly, if you plan to have a pool, this should be done before you start on your garden or many of your plants will be destroyed by workmen removing soil and dumping gear. New homeowners must be on their guard to see that the builders remove all rubble before leaving the site. Do not, under any circumstances, allow them to bury it on the property. Although it is their duty to take it away they are usually only too keen to spread it about the erf and then lightly cover it with soil. If you allow this to happen you will have untold trouble when you start planting, and the cost of removal at that point is exorbitant.

Once the permanent features have been taken care of it is normal to move onto planting trees which are planned to provide shade – and certainly those likely to take many years to develop.

Consider including among these that glorious member of the magnolia family – North America's *M. grandiflora*. This beauty will forever be a joy to you, for even as a very young plant it provides large creamy-white blooms. Don't, however, expect shade for many, many years. Sadly, these magnolias are so slow growing that you may never live to enjoy the full glory of yours, but don't be put off by this, they are beautiful at any age and will certainly always provide you with glorious blooms for interior decoration. One bloom makes an arrangement.

Having decided on your trees, whether for their flowers, foliage, shade or form, the next step is to plant screening material around the boundary and servants' quarters, or to conceal the compost heap.

Screening plants are generally a great

Hard to pronounce but a joy to work with, the fern-like Muehlenbeckia is a fast-growing shrub that produces masses of foliage cuttings for the arranger.

Magnolia grandiflora produces its magnificent large ivory-coloured blooms even as a small plant.

source of picking material; plants such as viburnums, photinias, privets, elaeagnus, eugenias and bottle brushes – are marvellous providers of cut foliage once they are established.

Plant these screening shrubs as soon as possible and ensure a variety of colours, such as greens and golds, some variegated and some plum-coloured. Try also to vary heights to avoid dullness and a hedge-like appearance and consider retaining views of attractive parts of your neighbour's garden and beyond.

A two or three metre-tall border may be perfectly adequate in most places and for this you can use fairly low-growing and even squat shrubs. However, there are bound to be places where you can vary heights: use narrower and loftier plants to obscure a neighbour's view from the window of a double-storey home or even of a telephone pole or lamppost that offends you. For these purposes Australia's glossy and beautifully berried *Syzygium myrtifolia (Eugenia)* is a delight, but you might even try one of the lovely conifers, *Cupressocyparis leylandii* or *C. torulosa* 'Compacta'. Although the conifer family is not of great use to the arranger, it is useful to have one or two in the garden for the odd snippet of greenery or the cones for Christmas decorations.

Plant densely by all means during this phase of your landscaping, but do not overplant; plant screeners as closely together as you can, but always bear in mind their eventual size. You must not, for instance, plant two shrubs in a space which is really only big enough for one.

Overplanting is one of the greatest curses in gardens, for too often you end up having to remove plants which have cost a lot of money or of which you have grown fond. Worst of all is the discovery on removing a plant that it has ruined, sometimes beyond recovery, the shape of neighbouring shrubs.

Admittedly it is very difficult to visualize a 30 cm-tall viburnum growing into a 3 m x 2 m monster in a matter of a few years but this is what happens. If you have planted a viburnum and a privet within a metre of one another, one or the other is going to have to give way.

It is wise to acquire a good gardening manual which gives you the eventual sizes of plants and these should be marked in on your plan before you put a spade in the ground. Once your plan is finalized, position your plants according to the measurements and stick to this arrangement. When you see two little plants standing metres apart, resist the temptation to jam in several more, or you will end up with a jungle of plants growing into one another, distorting the shapes of neighbours and losing shape themselves.

Recently I planted a muehlenbeckia in my fernery without checking on eventual size, thinking it would grow to the size of others I had seen. Then when passing a city park one morning I saw a real beauty which was several metres tall. Fortunately, I discovered my mistake before any damage was done – for it could have been a disaster. It was not at all suitable for the position I had chosen and would soon have swamped the beautiful holly and leather-leaf ferns which I had chosen as its neighbours.

Crowded gardens become tatty very quickly. Given proper planning and a little patience, however, your garden will very soon begin to look good and you will be able to cope in comfort – without having to remove any plants.

Should you be able to afford it or should

you be short on patience, then it will certainly pay you to buy large established plants. These are often available at good nurseries and by using them you will come close to producing the near miracle of an instant garden.

With your boundary secure, the next project on your agenda should be to shape your beds and herbaceous borders. It will not be necessary to plant these up immediately, but it is important to know where they will be positioned and how they will look, thus enabling you to get on with that all-important job of laying your lawn.

Creating the gentle curves needed for beds is best done with the aid of a hosepipe which has been softened in the sun. Make your lawn area as ample as possible; it will look bigger and better if unbroken by trees, shrubs or pathways, which give a bitty effect.

A rule of thumb used by many landscapers when planning a site is to give two-thirds of the property over to lawn, paved areas, patios and plantings around the house, and to retain the remaining third for trees and shrub borders.

Green 'floors' are a very attractive feature in a garden, but it is not necessary to go overboard on grass. There are in fact many areas, particularly those with low activity or in shade, where groundcovers may be used to great advantage. For the person aiming to have as much picking material as possible, many groundcovers provide an excellent supply. Among these are the lush growers such as the ivies, the variegated periwinkles (*Vinca major* and *V. minor*), as well as the easy to grow and always attractive Hen-and-Chickens (*Chlorophytum comosum 'Variegatum'*), also known as the spider plant.

Some groundcovers even provide flowers, such as the popular common English violet, the fragrant *Viola odorata*, and its Australian cousin, *V. hederacea* – a vigorous grower which produces masses of mini white and mauve violets. These prolific gems thrive in either dappled shade or sun.

Delightful for mini-arrangements are those colourful members of the carnation family, the many Dianthus varieties, such as Pinks (*D. alpinus*), 'Cheddar Pink' (*D. caesius*) and 'Brilliancy' (*D. deltoides*).

Although during your boundary plantings you probably included varieties that are not only useful for screening but also provide good pickings, it is when you start with the planting of your herbaceous borders that

you really get down to working with those many varieties of shrubs, perennials, bulbs and annuals which you have so patiently waited to plant for your vase.

Choose carefully, however, for there are many plants which do not take kindly to too much pruning and which never recover their shape or are extremely slow to do so. Avoid such plants as *Melaleuca armellaris*, waratahs, some of the proteas and *Banksia ericifolia* for anything but light pickings or you will ruin the symmetry of your border. Fortunately there are others such as elaeagnus, the cestrums, the flowering quinces, poinsettias and pussy willows, which seem to be totally unaffected by the theft of the odd branch.

When selecting your plants, ensure that you keep factors such as colour and contrast in mind, considering that some trees will provide leaves of yellow and gold, lime or silver, purple or even dark brown. Use them as an artist would, as part of an overall design, and use your principles of landscaping, do not merely dot plants about the place. You will find there are some excellent combinations, such as the dark leaves of plum, alongside the green-yellow of a golden elderberry, or the silver foliage of a cotoneaster with the dark green of an English laurel.

Most important when choosing your plants is the selection of only those that will survive your particular climate. It is pointless trying to grow tender *Ixora coccinea* if you live in cold Kroonstad, and roses hate the conditions near a beach. There are those plants which, given care, will grow in unlikely climates, but generally you will be doomed to frustration, even failure, and it is far better to go along with rather than fight the elements. If you are unsure what plants suit your area it is wise to visit a nearby nursery, where staff will know your conditions and be able to advise you. But you must also learn to be observant and study what grows in your neighbours' gardens. Pick out those plants which you know will thrive and plant them first, before you begin experimenting with what you think or hope might grow.

Visitors to garden centres often ask, 'When is the best time of year for landscaping my garden?' and if it is directed at me, my usual reply is: 'There is no time like the present!', but let me qualify this statement.

The 'present' time is not good if it is either extremely hot or cold. At other times, however, most plants – certainly those grown in plastic bags, suffer very little shock through transplant. In fact, if carefully done, they are unaware that they have been moved.

If you must work during times of extreme temperatures, then it is wise to take a few precautions. These can include spraying a plant in summer with one of the products on the market which reduces wilt due to transpiration. In winter, you might wrap a newly-planted tree or shrub in hessian to protect it against the cold.

If you are able to choose a time for landscaping, then autumn is a good time to get on with the job. The reason is that with the heat of summer past, the sun is no longer capable of scorching tender new growth, yet the ground is warm enough to encourage good roots to spread before winter sets in. If you carry out your major plantings of shrubs, trees and climbers before winter you will find that come spring the plants are established and just rearin' to grow!

With tender plants it is best to delay planting until spring, as this will give the plant a year in which to establish itself and to grow as big and strong as possible before the next winter sets in.

If you intend simply redesigning the garden, spring is the best time, for this is when plants are most easily and successfully divided. It is also a good time for doing any necessary transplants.

Should you inherit an established garden it is well to live with it for a year before digging it up and re-arranging it, for you never know what delights will turn up as the seasons change. In my own garden I was constantly surprised as the seasons followed one after the other. Unsuspected daffodils and St Joseph's lilies appeared and dry stems of a creeper on a fence developed into a mass of white blooms – a Chilean jasmine *(Mandevilla suaveolens)*. A very ordinary looking shrub which, on more than one occasion, I was tempted to dig out, was fortunately left to flower and turned out to be a fine Oxford and Cambridge bush (*Clerodendrum ugandense*), with its lovely two-tone blue flowers.

For the flower arranger a diary is vital when landscaping a garden. It should always be at hand to record when the foliage of a plant is looking its best and when certain flowers either come into bloom or fade. Times will vary from year to year, depending on the severity or mildness of the seasons, but a diary will certainly give you a reasonably accurate picture of when to expect certain species to 'perform'. Such information is particularly valuable when you need to plan flowers for an Easter wedding or a barmitzvah in the depths of winter.

It is important to record in your diary plants in your own garden and not to rely on information from gardens even a few blocks away, for micro-climates in different gardens can vary tremendously. Living on a

Snippets of conifer leaves add interest to this striking festive arrangement.

An unusual but delightful groundcover which offers a lovely shade of lilac-blue for small arrangements, from summer into autumn, is the humble *Plectranthus saccatus*. Although essentially a low-growing, shrubby plant, it will lift itself to more than a metre against a tree or wall and is exceptionally attractive rambling among other plants, particularly ferns.

In the vase it looks most attractive when arranged with its own leaves, with pink roses or in small mixed bowls, and if water is topped up regularly will keep in good condition for up to five days.

This and certain other varieties of these charming little plants also have leaves with many variegations, including yellow margins and blotches. Some are even tinged with pink. Fragrance is a bonus with some of them.

Most of these plants are hard to come by in nurseries and garden centres but keep your eyes open for they do appear occasionally. Certainly keep a watch on your friends' gardens, for you will find that most gardeners have one or other variety, and they are very easy to grow from slips, rooting even in a glass of water.

So small and dainty, the charming blue groundcover *Plectranthus saccatus* could easily be overlooked but it has obvious charms for the keen flower arranger.

hill, I have discovered that in my fairly frost-free garden such plants as my Chinese jasmine (*Jasminum polyanthum*) flowers a week or more earlier than in colder gardens in the valley, only a few hundred metres down the road. From your diary information it is possible to produce an orderly plan, which will simplify your on-going design from season to season.

Gardeners in townhouses or those with small gardens are often at a loss as to what plants they can grow successfully, but which will look attractive and be in proportion to their plot. It is safe to say that from the groundcover, annual and perennial divisions, you may choose practically anything to suit your taste and hobby and, except for large varieties such as the viburnums, you may use virtually any shrubs provided you keep them in trim.

It is possible to grow most creepers except for the exceptionally heavy vines such as the Cup-of-Gold (*Solandra guttata*) and *Beaumontia grandiflora*, and rampant creepers such as the banksia varieties. Some of the lighter creepers such as *Gelsemium sempervirens* and the jasmines are most suitable.

Trees constitute the main problem but even here there are a number of possible choices. Although your selection will be limited to trees that can provide flowers and foliage for your arrangements, there are still sufficient to landscape a lovely garden and have material for picking.

Small Trees
The following are among those most suitable for the arranger's needs:

Alberta magna
Camellia

Crab-apple (*Malus* varieties)
Dais cotinifolia
Dombeya varieties
Elderberry trees (*Sambucus* varieties)
Eugenia varieties
Flowering almond (*Prunus* varieties)
Flowering cherry (*Prunus* varieties)
Flowering gum (*Eucalyptus* ficifolia)
Flowering peach (*Prunus* varieties)
Flowering plum (*Prunus* varieties)
Frangipani (*Plumeria*)
Lilac (*Syringa* vulgaris)
Magnolia varieties
Maple varieties (*Acer* species)
Mountain ash (*Sorbus aucuparia*)
Penny Gum (*Eucalyptus cinerea*)
Protea varieties
Pride of India (*Lagerstroemia*)
Pussy willow (*Salix caprea*)
Silver tree (*Leucadendron argenteum*)

III *Your garden as a vase*

Placing material you particularly want in your landscape is the next step and a vital one in your plan. This is the 'arranging' of your garden and will probably be the biggest 'vase' you'll ever have to fill – so get it right!

It is most important that you concentrate as many of the plants you enjoy using as near to your work area as possible. If you use gypsophila regularly you won't want to have to run down to that bed at the front gate every time you make up an arrangement. Have it close to where you work. When you do your major pickings you will obviously roam your whole garden, but I suggest that you have as much of your foliage and filler material as close at hand as possible. Who, for instance, could live without a few bushes of asparagus fern or *A. plumosa* handy for the odd snippet?

Elaeagnus, a most attractive shrub and a wonderfully useful source of foliage material, is worth growing somewhere near the back door, as is the tough florist's fern. And why not include a bush of one of the abelias, with their lovely arching branches? If there is space you may even try a small tree such as the florist's or penny gum. Also useful would be a green or variegated ivy growing up a nearby wall or even thriving as a groundcover under a tree. The possibilities are endless and depend only on your requirements and taste.

Once again, when placing these plants, landscape with them – don't just pop them in willy-nilly. If you should decide to use one of the viburnums with their striking dark green leaves, for instance, then use it for what it is – a screener. Use it to block out a view of the washline or rubbish bin but at the same time bear in mind its eventual size, 3 m x 2 m. It is only suitable for a very large yard. If you must have it, find a not-too-distant place along your border where you need screening and plant it there.

Colour is something that may be spread throughout the garden. With today's trend towards low maintenance gardening, colour plants (annuals) are often used merely as features, near an entrance or as a

Elaeagnus – a must for the arranger's garden.

Only one 'Duftwolke' ('Fragrant Cloud') rose is needed to scent a room.

bright spot in view of the terrace. The vase-gardener will probably require more than the average homeowner, but the design principles are the same – placing bedding plants in front of foliage plants.

Many people today have swimming pools and the majority of homeowners in recent years have been tending towards a tropical look, using a number of large-leafed plants, such as strelitzias and philo-

dendrons, elephant ears and delicious monsters, which do not drop leaves in the water – but such plantings would be of little use to the average flower arranger. It is possible, however, to have a lush, cool-looking backdrop to the pool which also includes cutting plants. There are many of these and an excellent choice would be *Muehlenbeckia platyclados,* the fern-like shrub which many people refer to as the tape-worm plant be- 11 cause of the unusual jointed form of its leaves. Once it gets going this large, fast-growing dark green shrub will provide masses of filler material for your arrangements. Striking plants for pool areas are the flaxes, which have conspicuous leaves in a range of variegations, including the plum-coloured variety (*Phormium tenax* 'Atropurpureum'). Also of use are the many bamboos which vary in size, the great number of coprosmas with their lovely glossy green and variegated leaves, and shrubs such as photinias and fiddlewoods. Plants with useful and unusual foliage forms are the cat's tail fern (*Asparagus meyerii*), the various papyrus forms and the lacy sacred bamboo of Japan (*Nandina domestica*).

Cannas are fine perennials for pool and entertainment areas, whether clustered in bold beds or used to brighten backgrounds. They have in their favour lovely large leaves in a variety of colours from green to purple and even yellow. When in flower they provide bright splashes of colour and when without blooms their leaves offer strong contrasts. They are both excellent garden and arrangement plants, for even their seed-heads make useful additions to larger arrangements, once the flowers have faded.

For the flower arranger it is possible to use practically every corner of the plot for display material. Even the patio may prove a valuable source of supply if the walls and pergolas are put to good use. Patio walls may be draped in a variety of creepers which provide not only flowers and foliage but offer fragrance as well. Good choices would be the jasmines. Both the star jasmine (*Trachelospermum jasminoides*) with its Milky Way of flowers, against deep green foliage, and that harbinger of spring the Chinese jasmine (*J. polyanthum*), are ideal. Others would be honeysuckle, particularly the variegated form, which has yellow-green leaves; the Moonlight convolvulus (*Calonyction aculeatum*) – its flowers are lovely for dinner-table arrangements – and the Chilean jasmine (*Mandevilla suaveolens*).

If there are daughters in the family and future weddings are likely, then the garden should certainly host a stephanotis creeper. This fragrant beauty, with its lovely tubular blooms that are often called the 'bride's flower', is useful for all sorts of arrangements and should certainly be included in bridal bouquets. A spectacular creeper for the patio is that queen of climbers, the clematis. Boasting blooms in a wide range of colours and shapes, it offers the arranger not only flowers but also rather fun, swirling seed heads.

For beds, bowls and pots on the patio there are also hosts of different flowering and foliage plants which should be considered. Remember, however, that this should always be a light picking area or you will ruin the whole effect of your beautiful 'outdoor room'. A plump *Asparagus meyerii* may be robbed occasionally of one of its cat's tails without spoiling, and a flax or coprosma will not look any the worse for the theft of the odd snippet. Even a few petunias or azaleas nicked from that stunning bowl at the top of the stairs would probably go unnoticed.

Dare I suggest it – but even the play area could be bordered with some of the tougher plants and creepers you need for picking. The florist's gum (*Eucalyptus cineria*), a small silver-leafed tree which, while a marvellous weapon in the arranger's armoury, is not to my way of thinking the most beautiful of trees, could well be hidden in a corner of the children's playground. A tough English laurel (*Prunus laurocerasus*) would be a good choice as part of a screen dividing the area off from some other section of the garden. You could also have a border of abelias or privets and even a hibiscus or two would probably come to no great harm.

There's bound to be a rather windy corner somewhere about your erf and proteas love such spots, thriving on the buffeting. Plant a floriferous nodding pincushion (*Leucospermum cordifolium*). When fully grown it will produce many hundreds of flowers in a season, from which you may pick to your heart's content without diminishing its opulent circumference.

There are many other proteas from which to choose and what you settle for is very much a matter of taste – but the King protea

With their large and colourful leaves, ranging from yellow to green and plum, cannas are excellent contrast plants for the border and provide fullbodied foliage for the vase.

CLEMATIS

Fast gaining popularity in South Africa is the clematis, one of the delights of the English garden and surely one of the most beautiful creepers in the world – as attractive in the garden as it is in floral arrangements.

Little known until a few years ago when gardening personality Keith Kirsten started flying plants into the country on an annual basis for sale at his Waterkloof Garden Centre, the clematis is now proving itself, particularly in the cooler Highveld gardens.

Because of its rarity South African gardeners considered this queen among creepers difficult to grow, but this is not true, provided it is granted its few simple requirements. These are basically a good rich soil and a cool root run.

Clematis grows well in a variety of positions: against a wall, up a pole, through shrubs and trees, over pergolas or carports, on sheds, old trees and fences. The trick with clematis is to ensure that it is able to grow with its feet in the shade and its heads in the sun.

It is a voracious feeder and you should ensure it a good start in life when planting. Dig a square hole to a depth of at least 50 cm and into it mix a good potting soil or top soil, two buckets of peat and either well-rotted kraal manure or garden compost, ensuring that the manure is below the rootball of the plant. Two good handfuls of bone phosphate or SR 3:2:1 (28) fertilizer should also be added to the soil. If the soil is clayish or heavy, add river sand to ensure good drainage; clematis do not like wet feet.

A good idea when planting clematis is to place the rootball at least 2 cm lower than the soil level in the bag or pot, for this will allow for further stems to be produced from below ground level. It is even possible to cover clematis stems with soil for they root freely when buried, thus improving the plant's health and vigour.

Most importantly, ensure that the clematis roots are shaded, either by a neighbouring shrub or tree, or by wood-rounds, stepping stones or pebbles.

Watering is important and they should be given a deep drink every five days, or more often in really hot weather. Certainly they must never be allowed to dry out.

Ensure that the rootball is not disturbed when planting. Should the bottom roots encircle the pot or bag, loosen them slightly so that they will quickly grow out into the freshly prepared soil mix.

Do not despair in winter when leaves dry and the clematis stems look dry and dead. It is a deciduous plant and you will be rewarded in spring when masses of flowers burst out in a celebration of colour before the leaves appear.

Good varieties which are fairly common in South Africa today are 'Elsa Spath' (mid-blue), 'Hagley hybrid' (pink/mauve), 'Montana' (white), 'Montana Elizabeth' (soft pink), 'Nelly Moser' (pale mauve with lilac central bars), 'Niobe' (red) and 'The President' (purple/blue). A breathtaking sight is to see the two Montana varieties growing together with their flowers intermingling.

Of these the two best suited to flower arranging are 'Nelly Moser' and 'The President'. As cut flowers they last for about five days in cool weather. When picking choose only partially opened blooms on stout, fairly short stems, for those on weaker ones do not last nearly as long. Strip the leaves immediately and plunge the flower into cold water.

An added attraction of clematis is the fluffy whorled seed heads which also lend charm to arrangements.

(*P. cynaroides*), our national flower, is one of the easiest to grow and its spectacular giant blooms are always extremely useful for the special occasion. Other good choices are the oleander-leafed protea (*P. nerifolia*); the peach protea (*P. grandiceps*); the florists' favourite protea *P. longifolia* and even the common sugar bush (*P. repens*).

In addition to colour, texture, foliage, screening and all the other things one designs into one's landscape, fragrance must not be overlooked for its vital role both in the garden and in flower arranging. Half the charm of a vaseful of sweet peas is the scent and what could be more delightful than to stroll through a living room perfumed by tall St Joseph lilies.

In beds against the house it is worthwhile planting fragrant shrubs and climbers to scent bedrooms and living-rooms and there are many plants which may be used for this purpose which will also provide you with foliage and flowers for your arrangements. Among them is Yesterday, Today and Tomorrow (*Brunfelsia calycina* 'Eximia') whose small bright green leaves are a lovely colour for arrangements. Also useful for flowers and foliage is the coffee jasmine (*Murraya exotica*), while mock orange blossom (*Philadelphus coronarius*) offers delightful blooms and shepherd's holly (*Osmanthus ilicifolius*) provides shiny dark green holly-like leaves.

In warmer gardens frangipani (*Plumeria rubra*) is a delightful presence with its many-hued varieties, providing flowers over a long period in summer.

Take care when using fragrant flowers that their scent is not overpowering. For instance, one tuberose in a vase is quite sufficient even in a large room, while too much foliage of the herb rue in an arrangement could have many of your guests running for cover.

Certain rooms in the house call out for a fresh fragrance, particularly those that one passes through briefly, such as hallways and passages and particularly an entrance hall. Here one may use small arrangements of such charmers as lavender or mock orange blossom, a single hyacinth grown in a bulb vase or a 'Duftwolke' ('Fragrant Cloud') rose. For a guest toilet a tiny bunch of miniature roses, pinks – those lovely little mini-carnations – or a posy of sweet coffee jasmine shows thoughtfulness and a pride of home that invariably delights visitors.

The entrance to your home is important. Here you need a lot of eye appeal and this is a good position for those striking beds of annuals. Remember, though, that when they die and are removed, these beds can develop into ugly scars. It is thus a good idea to include in the beds some perennials or small shrubs, so that when the bold colour has passed its peak there are other plants to provide interest. For this focal position it is necessary to choose plants which will provide colour over as long a period as possible, such as the free-flowering *Lavatera trimestris*, nicotianas, marigolds and petunias for summer and ranunculus, anemones, calendulas and bush sweet peas for winter-spring. The advantage of such plants as ranunculus and sweet peas is that the more you pick them the more they flower – a flower arranger's dream. To prolong your display it is also always wise to plant your seeds or seedlings at weekly or fortnightly intervals.

There is a huge range of annuals for practically all seasons of the year available in nurseries and garden centres all over the country. Chat to a knowledgeable horticulturist there who will advise about long-lasting and free-flowering varieties and those suitable for splash colour as well as picking. New varieties of annuals are always being tried out by growers and your nurseryman will be able to tell you about them. Often plants such as Zinnia 'Envy', a green form of this annual which is much sought after by arrangers, are available on request. They may not be on the seedling racks but by chatting to your plantsman you may well find that there are all sorts of things which he may be able to order for you. Don't just accept what is on display, there are often interesting plants such as hybrid alstroemeria which, although not freely available, may be acquired for anyone especially interested.

One of the tricks of selecting plants suitable for the vase is to find as many as possible that don't spoil or lose shape with picking. Among them are the various abelias, once they are well established, roses which thrive on regular pruning, and certainly daisies.

It is worth mentioning that those gardeners who have the space available should develop a special hidden picking garden. In such a place you are able to grow for the vase those flowers which will provide you with quantities of blooms over a long period. If you can have a vegetable garden to cut down on bills, why not a picking garden?

In addition to the free-flowering varieties already mentioned you could add arum lilies and gladioli. Dahlias are flowers which I rarely find attractive in beds and borders, but they are useful for indoor decoration and may be grown in quantity, away from the gaze of visitors and passers-by.

Mrs Dora Peart, a well-known Pretoria garden designer over many years, once allowed me to see her magnificent picking

garden. In it she grew a great number of flowers, but what intrigued me most was her method of growing sweet peas. What she had done was to 'plant' dead branches of trees which had had their leaves removed and over these she allowed her sweet peas to ramble in profusion. The idea she admitted was not her own but one she had discovered during a visit to London, when she had been taken on a tour of the gardens at St James' Palace. 'There,' she said, 'it was necessary to have masses of flowers available for cutting at all times, for display in the rooms of the Royal residents.'

Sweet peas not only brighten our winter gardens but scent them and provide a mass of cut flowers for the home. And, a boon for the arranger, the more you cut the more they flower.

However, as with most things in life that are really worthwhile, you need to put in a little effort for real success. Sweet peas do demand a little more work than most annuals.

It is very easy if you just follow the programme:

Soil Being big feeders this is an important aspect and beds should be prepared a month in advance.
- Dig a trench 25 cm wide by 25 cm deep.
- Lift out the top soil and put on one side. Lift the bottom soil and reserve it on the other side of trench.
- Into the bottom soil work quantities of compost and well-rotted manure plus half a cup of super phosphate for each metre of trench.
- Into the topsoil also mix compost and kraal manure but here include half a cup of SR 3:2:1 (28) fertilizer for each metre of trench.
- One week before sowing seed, lightly sprinkle the trench with agricultural lime and rake it into the top soil.

Sowing Mid-March to April is the best time. Assist germination by soaking seed overnight. Handle wet seed with care.
- Sow 12 mm deep.
- Put some river sand in the bottom of the drills to facilitate drainage.
- Place light layer of compost or vermiculite over soil which should be kept cool and moist but not saturated.
- Protect with bird netting for it is the early bird which nips out those first tender green shoots as they appear above the soil.

Training Once the plants are 8 cm tall remove bird netting and for climbing sweet

An excellent idea for a picking garden is to grow climbing sweetpeas over branches which have been 'planted' into the ground.

peas replace with some form of trellis. For sweet peas in beds it is a good idea to make either wigwams with cane or cylinders with chicken wire.
- At this stage also pinch back young plants, retaining a few strong shoots which come from the base.
- Start training on to the trellis with plastic budding tape as soon as possible.
- Remove all side shoots and tendrils and once flowering keep picking flowers to prolong the blooming. Once allowed to go to seed sweet peas will stop producing flowers.

Feeding Plants should be watered copiously several times a week and once in bud should be fed fortnightly with a liquid fertilizer.

Some plants which are useful for decorating but which have an untidy appearance in borders and should be kept hidden are Honesty (*Lunaria annua*), with its lovely silver ten cent piece-like discs, *Statice latifolia* and gypsophila, both of which have baby's breath-like flowers. I would even go so far as to say that I believe that rose gardens are best kept hidden. Although I will admit that the rose is the most perfect of flowers, few rose gardens ever inspire me. Though rose fundis disapprove, I generally find that roses look their best when included in mixed borders with other plants.

Shade gardens are a problem for many gardeners, but these too can be put to good use by the enthusiastic flower arranger or Ikebana devotee. They will find useful the many varieties of flowers and foliage which enjoy a little protection from the hot sun. One of the most useful varieties requiring dappled shade is the coprosma, available in several forms and with leaves varying from plain dark glossy green (*C. baueri*) to the variegated forms: glossy green and yellow with speckles (*Coprosma* 'Marble Chips'); green with golden centre (*C. picturata*) and the shiny green with cream border 'Coffee Cream' (*C. baueri variegata*). These are all delightful shrubs, ideal for adding colour and contrast to the cooler parts of the garden while also providing useful foliage for the vase.

Other good shrubs for cool places are *Aucuba japonica*, with its yellow speckled leaves, and those acid-soil loving plants, azaleas, camellias and gardenias. Camellias and gardenias offer both flowers and attractive shiny dark green leaves that lend interest to arrangements. Clivias and agapanthus, arums and hydrangeas will also brighten and lighten your shade areas and provide quantities of interesting material for your vases.

SHADE GARDENS

Some useful plants for gardens with shade and semi-shade:

ANNUALS

Begonia
Canterbury Bell (*Campanula*)
Cineraria (*Senecio*)
Coleus
Columbine (*Aquilegia*)
Foxglove (*Digitalis*)
Impatiens
Lobelia
Mimulus cupreus
Pansy
Primula malacoides
Primula veris
Viola

BULBS

Amaryllis
Anemone
Arum

Begonia
Chincherinchee
Daffodil
Freesia
Galtonia
Grape hyacinth (*Muscari*)
Hyacinth
Iris (Dutch)
Ixia
Leucojum
Lilium
Monbretia
Tritonia
Tulip

CREEPERS

Delicious monster (*Monstera deliciosa*)
Honeysuckle (*Lonicera* varieties)
Ivy (*Hedera* varieties)
Star Jasmine

GROUND COVER

Ajuga reptans varieties
Dianthus deltoides
Ground polygonum (*Polygonum capitatum*)
Ivy
Wild strawberry (*Duchesnea indica*)

PERENNIALS

Agapanthus varieties
Arum varieties (*Zantedeschia*)
Blue Columbine (*Aquilegia alpinus*)
Bergenia cordifolia
Campanula glomerata
Day lily (*Hemerocallis*)
Ferns
Geum chiloense
Hosta
Jacob's ladder (*Polemonium caeruleum*)
Japanese anemones
Lenten rose (*Helleborus lividus* 'Corsicus')
Wild rhubarb (*Acanthus mollis*)

SHRUBS

Coffee jasmine (*Murraya exotica*)
Coprosma varieties
Flowering quince (*Chaenomeles lagenaria*)
Gardenia varieties
Ixora coccinea
Justicea (*Jacobinia*)
Japanese laurel (*Aucuba japonica*)
Mock orange blossom (*Philadelphus coronarius*)
Plectranthus
Plumbago capensis
Shrimp flower (*Beloperone guttata*)
Veronica (*Hebe* varieties)
Yesterday, Today and Tomorrow (*Brunfelsia floribunda*) and *B. calycina* 'Eximia'

SEASONAL SCENTED GARDENS

ANNUALS

Carnations – summer
Dianthus – spring/summer
Nicotiana – spring, summer, autumn
Sweet peas – spring
Sweet William – summer

BULBS

Freesia – spring
Hyacinth – spring
Lilium varieties – summer
Lily-of-the-valley – spring
Tuberose – summer

CREEPERS

Honeysuckle – spring
Jasmine varieties – late winter, early spring
Mandevilla – summer
Rangoon creeper (*Quisqualis*) – summer
Stephanotis – summer
Star jasmine (*Trachelospermum jasminoides*) – spring
Wisteria – spring

PERENNIALS

Bergamot – summer
Buddleia – summer
Forget-me-not – spring
Geranium (scented varieties, rose, lemon etc) – spring/summer
Lavender varieties – spring/summer
Pinks – summer
Violet – spring
Wallflower – spring

SHRUBS

Camellia sasanqua – autumn/winter
Cestrum – summer
Coffee jasmine – summer
Daphne – summer
Gardenia varieties – summer
Mock orange blossom – spring
Osmanthus fragrans – early summer
Rose varieties – spring/summer
Rothmania – summer
Spanish broom – spring/summer

TREES

Frangipani – summer, autumn
Magnolia grandiflora – summer
Mimosa (*Acacia* species) – spring

IV   Painting your garden canvas

Few pleasures in this world are as satisfying as growing things, no matter how simple they may be – a few marigolds or a row of radishes – and for the flower arranger the real thrill in gardening comes when you settle down to grow the colour you have always wanted. Colour is what makes a garden cheery and inviting, just as it is cut flowers indoors that make a home warm and welcoming and so 'painting' your garden canvas with blooms and blossoms is the fun part of gardening for the vase.

Annuals you will find provide the big show but bulbs offer an unmatched sense of excitement during spring and summer, while perennials give the garden a feeling of permanency.

These three categories of plants supply most of the colour in the garden and vase, and most certainly constitute the principal picking area for the arranger. Shrubs, trees and climbers mostly provide filler material, variety and texture.

For the home decorator the real joy of growing one's own flowers, whatever they may be, is that they add a freshness and an interest to arrangements which is often un-obtainable with bought flowers. The ephemeral nature of many of them makes them unsuitable for sale in a florist shop but ideal for a quick home arrangement – just a few flowers for a dinner party or a small vase for the room of an overnight guest. What could be more charming than Moonlight convolvulus blooms picked for your table moments before your guests arrive or some hibiscus enjoyed for their brief but glorious 24-hour life span?

Probably one of the most important facets of growing your own material is that you can specialize to the extent that you grow those flowers whose colours enhance your interior decorating schemes. How often have you rushed out to the flower sellers or the market to buy pale pink roses or pink al-stroemeria to find available only yellow and white chrysanthemums, red roses and red and white carnations?

For bold effect it is best to mass one colour in a bed, such as the popular 'Pineapple Crush' marigold, a low growing but large-flowered variety which is self-cleaning and provides a show for months in summer.

The larger your garden the more flexi-bility you will have in choosing annuals for your beds and borders, but whatever the size be most careful in your selection.

Certainly on a small plot you will have fewer beds, so the plants chosen will need to be the most floriferous available. Among them you will use such annuals as *Lavatera trimestris*, which give a splendid display for six to eight weeks at a time and which, like petunias, are suitable for both summer and winter planting. Then there are zinnias and

Labour intensive though they may be, bedding annuals like these are a spectacle that makes the time and trouble spent on them worthwhile. A colourful bed such as this is both a delight for those who see it and provides abundant pickings for the vase.

marigolds that flower all summer long. For spring, two winners are sweet peas and ran-unculus which last a long time and longer still if you keep picking. These are but a few and you will find in the lists provided a huge   17

variety of suitable plants in various colours.

Although colour is important, remember too when choosing your plants that their shape is also a major consideration. You will need rosette-type blooms, such as marigolds, zinnias and bedding dahlias, which come in a vast range of colours from yellow to purple; spikes and spires – such as snapdragons, larkspurs, delphiniums and penstemons; bells – foxgloves and Canterbury bells; star-like flowers – Gloriosa daisies, Namaqualand daisies and asters; plumes, tails and tassles – grasses, celosia and amaranthus; flats – zinnias; fluffies such as gypsophila and puffies such as cleomes.

Each spring and autumn garden centres and nurseries display a bewildering array of seedlings. The better ones offer trays with labels on them illustrating the flower and giving important details such as variety name, colour and mature height, plus the aspect needed for best growth. One thing that will not appear on the label and which, if you live in a frost area, you may need to know, is whether the plant is tender or hardy. This is something you should find out from your nurseryman.

Often the plant may be available in a variety of individual colours or in mixed trays. If not on display, ask one of the salesmen about the colour you require, for they may be only temporarily out of stock and it is quite likely that he will be able to order your particular colour. Plants such as petunias and nikkis, pansies and violas come in a wide range of colours.

When buying your seedlings, consider whether you need flowers for sunny areas or dappled shade. This is another item you can check on the tray label.

Height is most important. When planning your beds you will want to plant taller varieties behind the shorter ones for best effect, with really low growing varieties, such as lobelias and alyssum, up front as a border.

Before seedlings were so freely available most people used to buy seeds, and true gardeners would gather together a great variety of catalogues which they would study while planning their next season's beds and borders. What was particularly good about this system was that gardeners tended to be adventurous and would often try to grow plants they had never heard of and in this way discovered delights which made their gardens different from others in the neighbourhood.

The growth of the seedling business has in fact tended to a certain unfortunate uniformity in bedding plants. For interested parties, however, the day of seed catalogue ordering is not over – there are still many companies, both local and overseas, which send out marvellous colour brochures which are not only sources of supply but also of inspiration and delight.

If mail ordering is not for you, then visit your local garden centre and study the seed racks. There you will find a great variety of seeds of plants never seen among the trays of seedlings. And, should there be something you specifically want and which is not displayed, chat to the store staff. They will almost certainly be able to order what you want.

When planning your beds it is wise to use one colour if you want a bold effect. Even if you have limited space and want a variety of colours, it is more effective to have a number of small single-colour beds than to use mixed colour beds which give the

Zinnia linarifolia provide not only a bright display in the garden but make excellent cut flowers and also dry well.

Shapes and textures are as important as colours when it comes to flower arranging and the pictures above show some of the variations from spiky to fluffy and round, droopy and daisy-like. The range is almost endless.

A much underrated vase flower is the petunia which thrives so well in our South African gardens. When picking petunias you must be careful as they are frail, but other than that they are easy and last well in the vase. They continue to open in water over a period of several days, particularly if the water is changed. Here they are displayed in a tallish jar, with the dove-topped lid adding charm to the decoration.

White flowers are night flowers and show up particularly well by moonlight but they also brighten dull corners of the garden and add a light touch to a mixed border.

Petunias may be grown all year round but must have good drainage. Although excellent tub and windowbox subjects they must not become waterlogged. They enjoy climates with dry days so they do best in the Cape in summer and in the northern provinces in winter.

19

garden a splotchy appearance.

When buying your plants do try the newer hybrid varieties rather than the old-fashioned kind, for they can be counted on for vigour, uniformity of colour, size and growth habit, and very often outclass standard plants in the abundance of blooms they produce. This is especially the case with such plants as petunias, pansies, snapdragons, bedding begonias and zinnias.

Take care over the choice of plants – look for the healthy, clean, well-branched specimens with green leaves rather than leggy and yellowing plants.

Pinching back seedlings, nipping out the growth point, is most important and ensures a bushier plant. Although the first bloom is lost you are ensured of better looking plants which will go on to produce more flowers. Excellent examples of plants which thrive on this treatment are zinnias and petunias, which tend to become very straggly if not handled properly.

There are a few annuals that should not be pinched back, such as poppies, cockscomb and balsams, but they are few and far between and if in doubt check with the salesman when buying.

Proper drainage and preparation of the soil is most important when arranging your beds. Heavy fertilization is not necessary and can encourage leaf growth rather than flowers, but do dig over the soil well and include quantities of compost. It is wise to first loosen the soil to a depth of 15 cm and then to cover the entire area with a 5 cm layer of compost and work it in well. Some people like to include a light dressing of 3:2:1 (28) fertilizer, but a little superphosphate to encourage buds is also beneficial.

Watering of your seedlings is most important for the surface soil is the first to dry out and as their roots are not very deep they need to be watched. It is far better, however, to give an occasional good watering rather than a number of superficial sprayings. It is also wise to surround your plants with a few centimetres of organic mulch which helps to retain moisture, prevents soil compaction, reduces weeds and generally improves the appearance.

When the weather is very hot, cover your young seedlings with those small cardboard caps – rather like mini-umbrellas – which are available in all garden shops, or gently lay leafy branches among them to give them a little shade until strong enough not to need it.

Once your annuals are flowering it is important, if you do not pick them all, to remove dead heads. This not only makes for a neater appearance but in most cases encourages the plant to flower more. This is particularly true with such annuals as sweet peas, snapdragons, zinnias, pansies and calendulas.

NIKKIS

An excellent example of a new hybrid in recent years is the nikki, a shorter growing version of nicotiana (tobacco plant) which was lovely but rather leggy. The hybridists have now reduced its size by half – to 40 cm tall – and unlike the old-fashioned kind it stays open long and is much more showy. It is excellent both for the border – flowering right through the summer – and for floral arrangements.

Initially the nikki's colour range was limited but now, in addition to the pink, white and red, there is rose and a 'lime', an unusual and extremely useful green-yellow colour.

Nikkis are one of the easiest flowers for the vase, for they almost arrange themselves and require no more treatment than the removal of the lower leaves from the stems.

Pansies make a delightful small arrangement in this silver posy bowl. They need no treatment but are very thirsty and must be topped with water regularly. Pansies today come in a range of single clear colours – yellow, blue, white and even red.

Colourful annuals which are useful in specific areas, the situations in which they thrive and their seasons:

ALL-YEAR-ROUND

Alyssum
Lavatera trimestris
Lisianthus russellianus
Pansy*
Phlox
Petunia
Snapdragon (*Antirrhinum*)*

* For cold areas

WINTER/SPRING

Calendula*
Cineraria (*Senecio*)*
Iceland poppy*
Nemesia*
Pansy*
Penstemon*
Primula malacoides
Schizanthus (poor man's orchid)*
Stock (*Matthiola incana*)*
Sweet pea (*Lathyrus odoratus*)*
Viola*

HEIGHT

Amaranthus, 90 cm
Aster, up to 80 cm
Bells of Ireland (*Molucella laevis*) 75 cm*
Canterbury bell (*Campanula*) 70 cm*
Celosia, 70 cm
Cleome, 120 cm
Columbine (*Aquilegia*), up to 90 cm*
Delphinium elatum, 150 cm*
Foxglove (*Digitalis*), 90 cm*
Gloriosa daisy (*Rudbeckia*), 110 cm
Hunnemannia fumariifolia, 60 cm
Lavatera trimestris, 60 cm
Lisianthus russellianus, 60 cm
Marigold hybrids, up to 95 cm
Penstemon, 75 cm*
Salpiglossis, up to 90 cm
Salvia farinacea (blue salvia) 60 cm
Salvia splendens, up to 70 cm
Scabiosa, up to 100 cm*
Snapdragon (*Antirrhinum*), up to 100 cm
Zinnia, up to 90 cm

LOW BORDERS

Ageratum, 20 cm
Alyssum, 10 cm
Dianthus variety, under 20 cm
English daisy (*Bellis perennis*), 15 cm*
Marigold hybrids, 15 cm
Nasturtium, 15 cm
Primula malacoides, under 20 cm
Salvia splendens, 15 cm
Sweet William, 15 cm
Verbena, under 20 cm
Viola, 15 cm*

SHADY PLACES

Canterbury bell (*Campanula*)*
Cineraria (*Senecio*)
Columbine (*Aquilegia*)*
Clarkia
Forget-me-not (*Anchusa*)
Foxglove (*Digitalis*)*
Pansy (in summer)
Primula malacoides
Torenia
Viola*

WINDOW BOXES

Alyssum
Dianthus
Lobelia
Marigold
Nasturtium
Pansy*
Petunia
Phlox
Verbena
Viola*
Zinnia (small varieties)

HANGING BASKETS

Alyssum
Lobelia
Nasturtium
Nemesia
Pansy*
Petunia
Primula malacoides
Viola*

FRAGRANCE

Alyssum
Bells of Ireland*
Carnation
Heliotrope*
Nikki
Stock
Sweet pea*

WHITE-BY-NIGHT

Ageratum
Alyssum
Candytuft
Canterbury bell*
Carnation
Cineraria
Cleome
Gypsophila
Lavatera trimestris
Lisianthus russellianus
Nikki
Pansy*
Primula malacoides
Stock*
Viola

FOR DRYING (HANGING-UP)

Bells of Ireland*
Everlasting (both South African and Australian varieties – *Helipterum* and *Helichrysum*)*
Statice (all the *Limonium* varieties)*
Globe thistle (*Echinops ritro*)*

21

ANNUALS

The following annuals are worth growing in the garden for use in arrangements both big and small.

Name	Colour	Height	Aspect	Season
Ageratum	Blue, white, pink, violet	10–20 cm	sun	spring/summer
Alyssum (*Lobularia maritima*)	primrose yellow with silver foliage (perennial); purple, rose, white (annual)	10 cm	sun	all year
Amaranthus	red	90 cm	sun	summer
Antirrhinum (Snapdragon)	yellow, pink, copper, red	25–100 cm	sun	all year
Aquilegia (columbine – really a perennial)	cream, pink, yellow, blue, red, crimson	75–90 cm	shade	spring/summer
Aster	wide variety of colours (whites, pinks, blues, purples)	25–80 cm	sun	summer
Bellis perennis (English daisy)	white, pink, red	15 cm	sun	winter
Bells of Ireland	green	75 cm	sun	summer
Browallia	blue and white	50 cm	sun	summer
Calendula	cream, lemon, yellow, orange	30–50 cm	sun	winter
Calliopsis	yellow	50 cm	sun	summer
Campanula (Canterbury bell – a biennial)	white, pink, mauve, blue	70 cm	semi-shade	spring
Carnation	red, white, pink, yellow and bi-colours	50 cm	sun	summer
Candytuft (*Iberis umbellata*)	pink, lilac, rose, purple, white	25 cm	sun	summer
Celosia	golden-yellow, carmine, scarlet	70 cm	sun	summer
Cineraria	pink, red, lavender, blue, white, blush and bi-colours	40 cm	shade	winter
Clarkia	double flowers, salmon, pink, rose, mauve, purple, red, white	50 cm	sun/shade	summer
Cleome	rose, pink, lavender, white	120 cm	sun	summer
Cornflowers	blue, pink	30 cm	sun	spring
Dahlia (seed dahlias)	pink, red, yellow, white, orange, crimson	40 cm	sun	summer
Delphinium elatum (Pacific Giants)	blue, salmon, rose, lilac, purple	150 cm	sun	summer
Delphinium sinensis	azure blue	25 cm	sun	summer
Dianthus deltoides	red	20 cm	sun	summer
Dianthus sinensis	red, white, yellow, pink and mixtures	15 cm	sun	summer
Digitalis (Foxglove)	white, cream, yellow, pink, lavender, magenta, purple	90 cm	semi-shade	summer
Forget-me-not (*Myosotis*)	blue	30 cm	sun/shade	spring/summer
Gaillardia	cream, yellow, orange, red	45 cm	sun	summer
Gloriosa daisy	yellow, gold, mahogany, all with brown eyes	110 cm	sun	summer
Gypsophila	white and pink	30–45 cm	sun	summer
Hunnemannia fumariifolia (Mexican poppy)	golden yellow	60 cm	sun	summer

Name	Colour	Height	Aspect	Season
Lavatera trimestris	pink	60 cm	sun	summer
Linaria	multi-coloured range	25 cm	sun	summer
Lisianthus russellianus	blue, pink, white	45–60 cm	sun	all year
Lobelia	blue	15 cm	sun/shade	all year
Marigold (African)	orange, yellow	96 cm	sun	spring/summer
Marigold (French)	orange, yellow, bronze	20–30 cm	sun	summer
Marigold (Hybrids)	bright yellow, gold, red/gold, bronze	15–90 cm	sun	summer
Mimulus cupreus	red and yellow with spots	25 cm	shade	summer
Namaqualand daisy (*Dimorphotheca*)	white, yellow, orange	20–30 cm	sun	spring
Nasturtium	bronze, yellow, red, orange	15 cm	sun/shade	summer
Nemesia	white, yellow, bronze, pink, crimson	20 cm	sun	winter
Nicotiana	red, white, rose, pink, lime	40 cm	sun	summer
Pansy	purple, white, blue, red, rose, yellow and combinations	15 cm	sun/semi-shade	summer and winter
Penstemon	pink, red, scarlet, lavender, white, blue	75 cm	sun	summer
Petunia	white, violet, red, pink, blue, purple, salmon, yellow and various bi-colours	30 cm	sun	all year
Phlox	pink, red, white, salmon, yellow, scarlet, lavender and bi-colours	15–40 cm	sun	all year
Poppy	orange, white, yellow	50 cm	sun	winter
Primula malacoides	mauve, pink, white, purple, red	20 cm	shade	winter/spring
Salpiglossis	gold, scarlet, rose, crimson, mahogany, blue	60–90 cm	sun	summer
Salvia farinacea	deep blue	60 cm	sun	summer
Salvia splendens	red, bright red, scarlet	15–70 cm	sun	summer
Scabiosa	blue, rose, lavender, red, coral	75–100 cm	sun	summer
Schizanthus (poor man's orchid)	combinations of pink, crimson, violet, purple	40 cm	sun	winter
Statice	blue, lavender, rose, white, yellow	30–100 cm	sun	summer
Stocks	white, cream, pink, rose, violet, purple	30–50 cm	sun	winter
Sweet pea	white, red, blue, pink, rose, cream, purple	30–50 cm and climbing	sun	winter
Sweet William	red, pink rose/purple, white	15 cm	sun	summer
Torenia	bi-colour, purple, lilac	25 cm	shade	summer
Verbena hybrids (dwarf)	red, white, pink, rose, salmon	20 cm	sun	summer
Viola	purple, white, blue, red, rose, yellow	15 cm	sun/semi-shade	winter
Zinnia	orange, yellow, pink, bronze, apricot, rose, cream, green, violet	25–90 cm	sun	summer

V *Bountyful bulbs*

Heralding the spring after a long hard winter, bulbs have over the centuries provided man with one of his greatest joys. With the cheery colours of their flowers, the beauty of bulbs is that they poke their bright heads through the ground into the sunlight at a time when little else is stirring in the garden.

Many South Africans are deprived of this wonder of nature as there is a belief among our gardeners that bulbs are tricky – something which is entirely untrue. Our beautiful climate is, in fact, ideal for growing bulbs – but there is a secret. 'Water, water, water' is the chorus sung by successful bulb growers – professional and amateur alike.

'It's very difficult to drown a bulb but you can let it die of thirst,' says Mr Floris Barnhoorn, managing director of South Africa's Hadeco – the largest bulb company in the Southern Hemisphere and one of the largest in the world. 'Watering deeply and regularly is the first principle of successful bulb growing,' he says. With this being the case the next question is 'How much is enough?'

In nature most bulbs, whether summer, winter or spring flowering, come from areas where growing seasons are wet, so the important thing is not to water all the time but during their growing season. Too much water at other times and the bulbs will rot. A good guide to the quantity of water is given by Mr Barnhoorn, who says, 'In my own garden I water the flower beds every four days, leaving the sprinkler in the same place for 1½ hours'.

An important reason for not allowing bulbs to dry out is that each contains an embryo flower which, once dead, nothing can revive. If you leave home for a holiday in the middle of bulb-growing season and your plants are not watered, you will more than likely return to 'blind' bulbs. Another common cause of bulbs going blind is that gardeners, when planting them, often leave them lying in the sun. They should be kept covered and cool at all times until planted.

There are a variety of aids to save on water bills and still keep plants moist. Plant your bulbs in a 'soup plate' depression so that water can soak in, and keep a good mulch of compost on top of your bulbs to retain moisture. For shade-loving bulbs it is a good idea to include some peat in the soil, as this helps to retain moisture in light and sandy soils and eliminate excess water in heavy clay soils.

Having hopefully convinced bulb lovers of the need to water their plants it can be said with total conviction that bulbs may be grown anywhere in South Africa – and as successfully as anywhere in the world. It is interesting to note that so successful is South Africa in this field that today even Holland is supplied with bulbs from the Republic.

When planting remember that most bulbs do best in a moderately sandy, loose, friable soil – slightly acid, with a pH of between 6,0 and 6,8 – and the best time to feed bulbs is at planting time. Prepare your beds in advance of planting by working over the soil to a depth of 30 cm, then cover with a 5–8 cm layer of compost and work into the soil.

Fertilizing is not really necessary but a slow-acting, long-lasting source of phosphate such as bone phosphate can only be beneficial in building up the root system – a suitable rate being about 3 kg to 12 sq m or 20 ml per bulb hole.

After bulbs have finished flowering they should be fed regularly to build up flowering potential for the following season – particularly if you plan to lift them. This is most conveniently done by using a good liquid

Bulbs in a mixed border provide a spectacular display but are best grown in single colour groups. This bright bed shows off a wide range of spring bulbs, including strelitzia at the back of the bed, three different coloured irises, a variety of narcissus including daffodils, hyacinth varieties, anemones, ranunculus and tulips.

Daffodils are a wonderful celebration of spring.

Liliums are available in a wide range of colours. Two popular varieties are 'Golden Trumpets' and 'Pink Perfection'.

Anemones, like ranunculus, flower long and freely. The more they are cut the more they bloom. Lovely flowers for the vase, they are best cut when buds are about to burst and colour is just beginning to show.

fertilizer. Bulbs to be lifted should be allowed to die down naturally. The dead leaves should then be cut off and the bulbs stored in a dry medium such as vermiculite until the following season.

It is important to buy good bulbs when planting – rather purchase fewer than a lot of inferior quality bulbs. Choose bulbs that are firm – never flabby, or with soft spots, bruises or blemishes.

It is never necessary to soak bulbs before planting – merely soak the soil thoroughly once they are in the ground and then keep them moist after flowering, until leaves start to wither.

There are essentially two periods of the year for growing bulbs: autumn, for spring flowering bulbs, and spring, for summer flowering bulbs. It is all a matter of temperature – a drop in soil temperature stimulates the growth of spring flowering varieties and a rise in temperature the growth for summer. Your local garden centre will be able to advise you on the correct time for planting bulbs in your area, but a general guide for spring-flowering varieties is March for the chilly Free State and Transvaal Highveld, while gardeners in warmer regions such as Pretoria, Cape Town and the Natal Lowlands should wait until April. For most summer-flowering bulbs the best time for planting is August – September, although liliums are usually ready in garden centres from May.

It is important for beginners to realize that bulbs should be 'planted', not 'buried'. A general rule is that there should be the same amount of soil above as the depth of the bulb itself. Two exceptions are liliums and gladioli, where the soil should be double the depth of the bulb.

The advantages of grouping bulbs together in depressions where they do very well, is that the 'water, water, water' rule is not the problem it at first appears, for in this way you concentrate your watering in limited areas.

For effect, when planting bulbs, it is better to plant groups of single colours, rather than mixed colours, except for ranunculus, anemones, freesias and sparaxis. Grouping separate colours is particularly important with hyacinths, for the different colours flower at different times which gives a mixed bed a patchy effect.

Bulbs can be used in a great variety of positions in the garden – in flower borders and rockeries, between shrubs and under trees, even in lawn and under groundcovers – giving a charming effect as they poke their heads through the ground.

For plants such as freesias, which are inclined to be floppy, it is a good idea to plant the bulbs in between shrubs or behind shallow walls where they will be protected from buffeting winds, otherwise it is necessary to stake them or to support them with thin wire.

Bulbs are at their best planted in clumps intermingled with annuals and perennials so that when they die down ugly gaps are not left in the border. The smaller the garden the more important it is to clump them together.

Bulbs also have many uses on stoeps and patios – even indoors, where they can save you an arrangement. Tulips, daffodils and hyacinths all look particularly good in troughs, tubs, bowls and windowboxes, while trailing tuberous begonias are spectacular planted in baskets.

A good idea when planting bulbs in containers is to use the treated varieties (hyacinths, tulips, Dutch irises), for these will pop up and flower at specially controlled times. Tulips, for instance, are available in May, June and July and should be planted as soon after purchase as possible – certainly within 10 days – and under average conditions they will flower 100 days later.

Treated bulbs are in fact excellent in the

Fragrant freesias are one of the joys of the spring garden but are best crammed in among other plants for support, otherwise they are inclined to flop over.

BULBS SUITABLE AS CUT FLOWERS:

	Bulb name	Common name	Flower colour
○○	*Allium cowanni*	florist's allium	white
○○	Anemone	anemone	purple, red, blue, white
○○○	Daffodil/Narcissus	daffodil	yellow, orange, pink white
○	Dahlia	dahlia	great variety
○○	Dutch iris	Dutch iris	blue, yellow, white
○○	Freesia	freesia	blue, red, yellow, white
○○	Gladiolus	gladioli	great variety
○	Hippeastrum	Amaryllis	red, pink, striped, white
○	Hyacinth	Dutch hyacinth	blue, pink, white
○○	Ixia	wandflowers	all colours mixed
○○	Liatris	gayfeathers	purple
○○○	Lilium	lilies	many colours
○	Monbretia	montbretia	orange
○	Muscari	grape hyacinth	blue
○○	Nerine	nerine	pink
○○○	Ornithogalum	chincherinchee	white
○	*Polianthes tuberosa*	tuberose	white
○	Ranunculus	ranunculus	many colours
○○	Tulipa	tulip	red, yellow, pink, white
○○	Zantedeschia	arum lily	pink, white yellow

○	good cut
○○	very good cut
○○○	excellent cut

garden and ideal for the flower arranger, for they flower a month earlier than regular bulbs, although they are planted later. They also generally grow taller and the blooms last longer. It is of interest that treated bulbs, even hyacinths, may be planted in full sun.

A smart way of saving on an arrangement is to grow hyacinths in those special glass hyacinth vases available today. They look magnificent in the clear glass vase with the bulb resting in a bowl at the top, while the roots hang through the stem to spread in the base of the vase.

At the end of the season it is best to lift your bulbs. This is done only when the leaves start to turn yellow. Daffodils and hyacinths may be lifted in November or December regardless of whether their leaves are still green as these can be snipped off later, once they have dried.

Many varieties of bulbs are available and the keen grower should experiment with some of the more unusual ones such as ixias and liatris, but for the average gardener there are numerous old favourites that will give little trouble and a tremendous amount of joy. These include tulips and hyacinths, ranunculus and anemones, sparaxis and freesias, plus the whole range of the Narcissus family, which includes daffodils and jonquils. An old favourite which is a must for the vase but which seems to be fading from the bulb racks of garden centres and nurseries is the montbretia.

Two varieties which seem to have lost favour with the general public but which are still popular with arrangers are dahlias and gladioli. Gladioli are very rewarding for

Dahlias with their bold colours and varied shapes – cactus, rosette and pompon – plus long strong stems – are ideal flowers for the vase and remain popular with arrangers.

Bulbs naturalized in lawn provide a brilliant display in this Florida garden. Probably South Africa's most enthusiastic bulb grower, Mrs Marjorie McLeod opens her garden to the public in spring in aid of charity and when in full bloom it is breathtakingly beautiful. 'My spring bulbs provide colour for many months, starting usually on my birthday, July 15, when a dozen or so daffodils make an early appearance,' says Mrs McLeod. 'Then in summer the bulbs are all mown down and I have a beautiful lawn.'

Among the easiest and most rewarding of bulbs are daffodils, which remain in the ground happily for many years, producing beautiful blooms for the vase each spring. They may be used either alone or in bold mixed bowls and suit a great variety of containers, from brass (as above) to ceramic, baskets and particularly clear crystal cylinders, which show off their lovely stems to advantage. Daffodils last well in the vase and if cut when buds are just opening will last even longer. They require very little water, only two or three centimetres, so for a mixed bowl should be added last.

they start flowering 90 to 100 days after planting, while dahlias with a little care produce masses of flowers. The best way to encourage flowering is to pinch back the growing points at the first stem joint in order to induce bushing. If particularly large blooms are required, remove some of the buds to allow fewer but larger blooms to form.

Many arrangers complain that bulbs do not last as well as other cut flowers but in fact this is probably their own fault. If vases are clean, really clean, flowers last for a long time and it is not necessary to add sugar or aspirin, Seven-up or anything else to keep them going. Expert grower, Floris Barnhoorn says, 'Vases should be kept even cleaner than your socks and underwear. If you put flowers in a dirty vase, bacterial action from previous arrangements will start breaking down the plant cells, thus shortening their cut lifespan. Always use washing machine bleach to clean vases – it kills bacteria very effectively.'

If cleaning vases with bleach is too much for you, those of you who have automatic dishwashers will find that they sterilize glass and ceramic ware perfectly.

FLOWERING CALENDAR

Autumn-planted bulbs bloom during:

July: Treated daffodils, treated Dutch irises, treated hyacinths, treated tulips.

August: Anemones, daffodils, Dutch iris, freesias, hyacinths, ranunculus, treated daffodils, treated tulips.

September: Alliums, anemones, daffodils, Dutch iris, freesias, hyacinths, ixias, liliums (early flowering – planted June/August), muscari, ranunculus, tulips.

October: Ixias, liliums (planted June/August), ornithogalum, ranunculus.

Spring-planted bulbs bloom during:

October: Amaryllis (plant six weeks before), early liliums (Umbellatum type).

November: Amaryllis (plant five weeks before), gladioli*, lilium, zantedeschia.

December: Amaryllis (plant five weeks before), gladioli*, liatris, lilium, zantedeschia.

January: Amaryllis (plant four weeks before), gladioli*, liatris, lilium, zantedeschia.

February: Dahlia, gladioli*, montbretia, nerine, tuberosa.

March: Dahlia, gladioli*, montbretia, nerine, tuberosa.

April: Dahlia, gladioli*, nerine.

* Gladioli should be planted successively – they take 90 to 100 days from planting before flowering.

Choosing the right bulbs when buying is important. They should look as firm and attractive as those in this display. They should never be soft, bruised or have blemishes of any kind.

The edge of a steep terrace wall is softened by a mixture of spring annuals and bulbs – sparaxis, freesia and ranunculus.

Flowering calendar of flower bulbs

To be planted in autumn, in bloom during

July
"Treated" Daffodils
"Treated" Dutch Iris
"Treated" Hyacinths
"Treated" Tulips
Strelitzia
*NB. "Treated" Hadeco bulbs are available from all leading nurseries and seed stores only during May.
*Strelitzia are generally sold as one-year- old plants and only start flowering after the 4th year.

August
Anemones
Daffodils
Dutch Iris
Freesias
Hyacinths
Lachenalia
Leucojum
Ranunculus
"Treated" Daffodils
"Treated" Tulips
Strelitzia

September
Alliums
Anemones
Daffodils
Dutch Iris
Endymion (blue bells)
Freesias
Hyacinths
Ixias
Lachenalias
Leucojum
Early flowering Liliums (plant June/August)
Muscari (Grape hyacinth)
Ranunculus
Sparaxis
Strelitzia
Tritonias
Tulips

October
Ixias
Lilium (plant June/August)
Ornithogalum (Chincherinchee)
Ranunculus
Strelitzia
Tritonias

Winter and Spring Flowering Bulbs and Tubers

Semi shade

Loosen all soil to a depth of 20 cm.
After planting provide a mulch of 1 to 3 cm thickness on top of the soil.
Plant slightly deeper than indicated if soil is very sandy.

Mulch: 1 to 3 cm

(10 x 10) = Spacing between bulbs in cm or distance from other plants in cm.

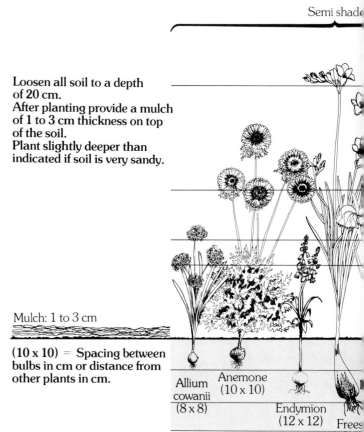

Allium cowanii (8 x 8)
Anemone (10 x 10)
Endymion (12 x 12)
Frees (10 x

Flowering calendar of flower bulbs

To be planted in spring, in bloom during

October
Amaryllis (plant 6 weeks before).
Chlidanthus
Early Liliums (Umbellatum type)
November
Amaryllis (plant 5 weeks before).
Chlidanthus
Gladioli*
Lilium
Zantedeschia (Arum Lily)
December
Amaryllis (plant 5 weeks before).
Galtonia (Berg Lily)
Gladioli*
Liatris (Gay feather)
Lilium
Tigridia
Zantedeschia
Zephyranthus
January
Amaryllis (plant 4 weeks before).
Begonia
Galtonia
Gladioli*
Liatris

Lilium
Tigridia
Zantedeschia
Zephyranthus
February
Begonia
Dahlia
Gladioli*
Montbretia
Nerine
Tuberosa
March
Begonia
Dahlia
Gladioli*
Montbretia
Nerine
Tuberosa
April
Dahlia
Gladioli*
Nerine
Strelitzia – flowers from April till October

*Gladioli should be planted successively, they take 90 – 100 days from planting till flowering.

Summer and Autumn Flowering Bulbs and Tubers

Full shade or semi shade

Loosen all soil to a depth of 20 cm.
After planting provide a mulch of 1 to 3 cm thickness on top of the soil.
Plant slightly deeper than indicated if soil is very sandy.

Mulch: 1 to 3 cm

(10 x 10) = Spacing between bulbs in cm or distance from other plants in cm.

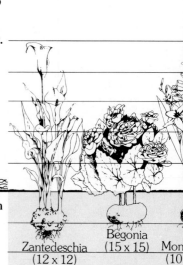

Zantedeschia (12 x 12)
Begonia (15 x 15)
Montl (10 x

Plant these during Autumn. Lift these bulbs during November. Store dormant bulbs in your garden shed or garage.
Illustrations not to scale

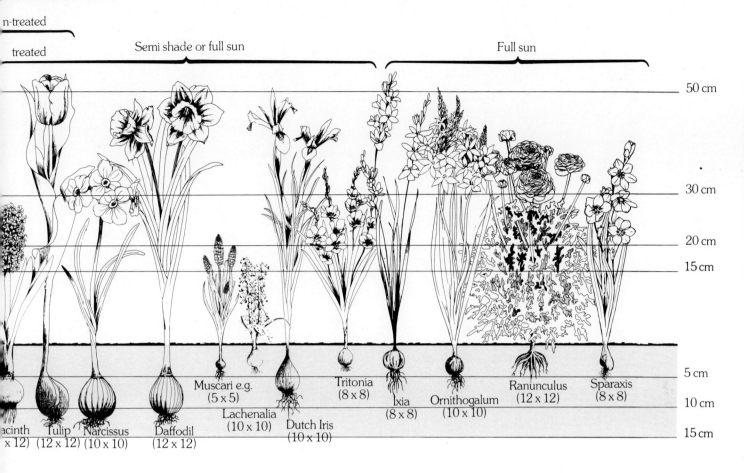

n-treated

treated

Semi shade or full sun

Full sun

50 cm

30 cm

20 cm

15 cm

5 cm

10 cm

15 cm

Muscari e.g.
(5 x 5)

Lachenalia
(10 x 10)

Tritonia
(8 x 8)

Ixia
(8 x 8)

Ornithogalum
(10 x 10)

Ranunculus
(12 x 12)

Sparaxis
(8 x 8)

acinth
x 12)

Tulip
(12 x 12)

Narcissus
(10 x 10)

Daffodil
(12 x 12)

Dutch Iris
(10 x 10)

Plant these during Winter and Spring. Lift these bulbs during May. Store dormant bulbs in your garden shed or garage.
Illustrations not to scale

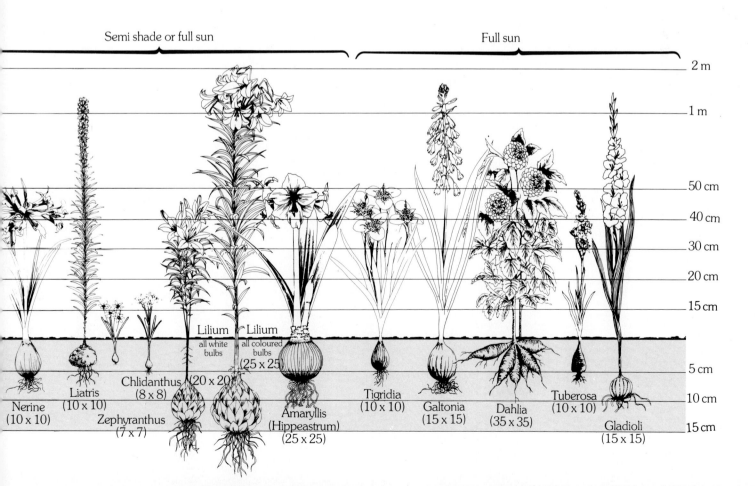

Semi shade or full sun

Full sun

2 m

1 m

50 cm

40 cm

30 cm

20 cm

15 cm

5 cm

10 cm

15 cm

Lilium
all white
bulbs
(20 x 20)

Lilium
all coloured
bulbs
(25 x 25)

Chlidanthus
(8 x 8)

Tigridia
(10 x 10)

Galtonia
(15 x 15)

Dahlia
(35 x 35)

Tuberosa
(10 x 10)

Nerine
(10 x 10)

Liatris
(10 x 10)

Zephyranthus
(7 x 7)

Amaryllis
(Hippeastrum)
(25 x 25)

Gladioli
(15 x 15)

31

VI *Dependable perennials*

Dependable colour that comes back year after year with very little help from anyone is supplied by perennials – known in gardening circles as the backbone of the border.

A simple definition of a perennial is 'Any plant that lives for more than a year', but to be more specific it is generally considered as one with herbaceous rather than woody stems and with leaves that may or may not die back in winter, but whose roots survive for many years. Typical examples are peony, the lovely plume-topped grasses, agapanthus and red hot poker.

Even during times of drought, when there is not much water for annuals, perennials still come up looking bright and beautiful. Although without water they may not flower for quite as long as they would normally, they still put on their annual display. Some, such as clivias and strelitzia, were never showier than during those dry early years of the 1980s – proving that we are inclined to overwater many of our indigenous plants in normal rain years.

Each season has its own reward and perennial colour is used in many instances for continuity and as a back-up to blooming annuals and bulbs.

To manage this effectively it is important to plan your combinations, considering not only the colour, texture and contrast of the plants but also their height and size, ranging the plants from tall at the back down to small and low at the front of the border. You must also think of their shapes, including some spires, some rounds, some misty and some bold, and of course never forget that the plants are for picking and to use in the sort of mix that will also be useful when it comes to designs for your vases.

Everyone develops their own favourite plant combinations for the border and this is where your diary and calendar will help a lot with your planning. The sort of 'arrangements' suitable for your beds are drifts of white Shasta daisies, backed by tall deep blue delphiniums and perhaps some bold, purple-leaved cannas, with a bright patch of

Indigenous clivias, proven drought fighters, grow well in the garden under trees or in tubs on patios.

Plumes of perennial grasses add interest to the garden, preserve well and play an important role in softening dry arrangements.

Gardens are not just made up of flowers – character comes from a blend of many things and most important are textures and colour. Here we see a striking mix of silver, gold and pink, with grasses, unusual leaves and spiky flowers.

33

'Lemon Drop' marigolds in the foreground.

Remember the aim is to have each plant either enhancing and complementing its companions, or a contrast of bold blooms with the fine and frothy, such as striking large cyclamen-pink cactus dahlias with a bush of the soft pink miniature daisies and their feathery grey-green leaves, surrounded by a sea of the cerise-rose Wonderland alyssum.

A good mix for a shady area could be bush fuchsias, with their pinks, purples and reds, accompanied by pink or white Japanese anemones, with blue *Plectranthus saccatus* and pale pink begonias pointing up the colour combination.

Arum lilies near a shaded pond look superb when partnered by tall blue agapanthus, columbines with their lovely maidenhair-like leaves and a low foreground of deep blue lobelia and pale-pink miniature impatiens.

For a bright sunny spot, day lilies blended with tall rudbeckias and yellow yarrow are a delight, as are white or blue irises mixed with pink perennial phlox, and pyrethrum (*Matricaria*), that game little white daisy with beautiful yellow-green leaves, combined with a fronting of the small bell-like pink flowers of the indigenous mini-perennial *Diascia integerrima*.

Cannas with their variety of leaf colours, from softest green to darkest bronze, are among the most useful of perennials in the garden, providing not only flowers but boldness, a change of texture and for the vase a fund of flower and foliage material.

Shade perennials are most important, particularly impatiens, which adds colour to an area where green is dominant. Even here, however, it is possible to add interest by using contrasting leaf shades and textures – the yellow-green Spider plant (*Chlorophytum comosum* 'Variegatum'), bronze ajuga and lush green of Elephant ears.

34

Also ideal for the sun are mini blue and white agapanthus which flower on and off throughout spring and summer, combined with yellow and blue irises, and lavender scabiosa interspersed with clumps of mauve garlic plant and deep-blue Japanese plumbago. This last mixture could also be lightened by red or salmon pink day lilies with a foreground of misty blue catmint.

These are the sort of combinations which make a border and with time and experience you will develop a variety of them. You will also learn to grow plants with overlapping blooming periods, in order to achieve the continuous kaleidoscope of colour every gardener dreams of. Most of all one learns that beds don't need to scream with colour, gentle blends are usually far more effective.

Although many people make up their borders with nothing but perennials and a few annuals, it is a good idea, where you have the space, to include a few long-flowering shrubs, such as plumbago, which goes on forever or a bright *Abelia* 'Francis Mason' with its yellow-green leaves and charming white blooms, or a flowering quince (*Chaenomeles lagenaria*), which puts on its display in winter when little other colour is in evidence. These are not used as accent plants or focal points but rather as an anchor around which the bed may be developed.

If your beds are narrow and you cannot use a shrub, try some standard roses, such as 'Iceberg' or 'Freesia', which are not only floriferous but which flower almost constantly from spring until pruning in late July.

Planning does not only mean the mixing of colours, shapes and sizes. There are other important considerations especially for the flower arranger. Most important when out cutting your blooms is easy access to your beds, so don't jam them hard against fence, fountain, or firmly in front of hedges or hot walls. It is always a good idea to leave a little space for use as a path between borders and such 'fixtures'.

Paths allow air to circulate around your plants, as well as providing space for roots to grow. This is important for a variety of reasons, including the fact that often plants are so closely packed that bottom leaves start turning yellow and in no time your borders take on an ugly, tired look. One also needs space to work, both for tidying up beds and for picking, so it is a good idea to place the odd wood-round or stepping stone among plants for easy access.

An additional problem with having plants too close to a wall, particularly if the wall is white, is reflected heat. This can be tough on both plants and blooms. Not only will it make them wilt but also cause them to flower and fade far more quickly than necessary.

Perennials have many benefits for the gardener but probably the most important is their labour-saving potential. Once planted they need little in the way of attention other than watering and occasional 'dead-heading'. This is to keep the bed looking tidy and in some cases, as with Michaelmas daisies, Shasta daisies and delphiniums, to induce more flowers. Constant removing of flower heads is also important to prevent them going to seed and thus weakening the plant.

Once established most perennials may be left where they are for many years, until the bed gets so overcrowded that it is time to divide clumps. This of course gives you more plants for other beds.

When dividing up old plants discard poor varieties, which have not flowered well and the mother plants which have done their

Chrysanthemums, with their lasting qualities as cut flowers have long been a firm favourite of gardeners for the vase and an excellent way of gathering together a collection of them is to buy individual pots at garden centres. There are many varieties such as this delightful bronze. The pot will give you pleasure in the home for many weeks and when the flowers die down, cut back severely and plant in the garden.

duty. Reserve for relocation the vigorous and fresh young plants from the outside of good clumps.

To divide a clump lift with a fork and either carefully pull the plant apart or, if necessary, separate with two forks and then try to disentangle the roots as carefully as possible.

Once separated trim and tidy the plants by cutting back the leaves with a sharp pair of secateurs, and don't be afraid to reduce root length to 10 or 12 cm. This will induce new and vigorous growth when replanted.

Perennials may be separated at virtually any time if you need to redesign a bed or border, but the best times for this work are generally in early autumn or spring.

When re-doing your beds include a few new varieties as this provides not only a change of scene but a greater choice of picking material.

Because perennials remain in the ground for such a long time it is most important that the soil in your beds should be well-prepared before planting.

Start by digging over the entire area to a depth of at least 15 cm and include in it as much decomposed material as possible – compost, old kraal manure or peat – and give the soil a dressing of fertilizer – preferably a slow-acting and long-lasting variety

Viola hederacea, the fast spreading Australian violet, makes a lush and attractive groundcover.

VIOLETS

Small but highly decorative and fragrant, English violets start peeping out from behind their dark green leaves at the end of winter and are extremely useful for small arrangements.

They are almost impossible to arrange and do not last if left singly, but if firmly bound together in the form of a posy, surrounded by their own leaves, they not only last well but look singularly attractive.

Once bound – this may be done with an elastic band or string but cotton is the best – stems should be trimmed to suit their container and put into water up to their necks. One bunch in a vase is super, but several small bunches in a deep posy bowl are a sensation.

In the accompanying arrangement the old-fashioned purple violets have been placed in a small pink lalique-type vase and used as a decoration to accompany a gift covered in lilac coloured paper. Adding to the charm of the arrangement, is the use of the Australian violet, a lilac and white mini groundcover (*V. hederacea*), to decorate the top of the parcel. Two glasses of champagne complete the arrangement.

Growing violets is fairly simple – for they will endure a lot of neglect, but given love and attention they respond by growing profusely. They need plenty of water and should be well fed with a liquid food in June and July.

Violets are best separated in November. If the clump has become unmanageable, retain only the vigorous outer shoots and discard the parent plant.

Plant your violets in good garden soil containing a lot of compost and some bone phosphate. Given the right conditions – that is not too hot – they will flourish and flower through July, August and September.

Violets come in a variety of colours, ranging through pale pink and pink to blue, a true violet and a deep purple – the one most commonly seen.

Demanding little from life, the *V. hederacea* is one of the finest groundcovers available, boasting both attractive leaves and charming small flowers over a long period and will grow in both sun and shade, looking good all year round.

Two different violets are used in this arrangement, the flowers of the lilac and white mini Australian violet, to decorate the gift while the old English favourite, the purple *Viola odorata*, is seen in the vase. The presentation is so lovely one can only wonder if it was worth spoiling the arrangement to open the gift.

such as bone phosphate or super phosphate. Work this in well.

Your best effects in the border are gained by using your palette boldly. Aim for sweeping banks of single varieties grouped together; avoid a patchy effect. Always use several plants in groups of threes, fives, sevens or even larger uneven number combinations. Try not to dot individual plants about willy-nilly.

As an artist works with colour, so you will learn that oranges and reds give a warm effect, silvers soften bright neighbours, yellow and particularly white show up well at a distance and on a moonlight night may produce breathtakingly beautiful displays. The brighter colours are best separated by paler neighbours, while greys and blues produce a cool effect.

Perennials include a wide range of plants and an aspect that must not be overlooked is the importance of herbs. These may be cultivated together in special herb borders or even gardens, but they also work in happily in your normal beds and borders.

Rosemary bushes and lavender, for instance, may be used in many positions. Yarrow is also bright and cheerful, while tall angelica with its lovely large flower-heads does well at the backs of borders. Very effective is the combination of yellows, such as irises and day lilies with a foreground of santolina, accentuated by the red plumes of celosia and a large clump of catmint with its lilac flowers and silver-blue leaves.

Groundcovers, which are really small perennials, are not only important in the garden scheme but may provide useful picking material and should also be carefully selected. A perfect example is ajuga. In addition to its great variety of leaf colours this busy little plant also produces spikes of clear blue flowers which make wonderful small country-style decorations.

Unfortunately some of the most useful and colourful groundcovers in the garden are not suitable for the vase as their flowers only open in sunlight. Among these are the various gazanias, trailing gazanias and the pink, white and yellow oxalis, but this should not stop you from including them in your border design.

For the purist who only wants cutting material, however, there are many charming and useful little plants such as the violets (*Viola hederacea*), the mini mauve and white

variety, and the popular fragrant English violet (*Viola odorata*).

Listed below are a few perennial plants which no flower arranger's garden should be without:

Agapanthus

This many-varietied indigenous beauty not only ranges through a great many blues, from pale to dark, but also offers a white in either large or dwarf size. Hardy and evergreen it grows best in full sun but will also flower well in semi-shade.

Although drought-resistant, it flowers best when well watered during its blooming period from late November onwards for a long spell. A thriving agapanthus will produce single spikes up to a metre in length with as many as 60 florets per umbel. Some dwarf varieties grow no larger than 25 cm tall, but the most common of the smaller growing types is usually about 50 cm tall. As they flower over the Christmas period they are extremely useful to the flower arranger.

Agapanthus (*A. umbellatus*), known as the Lily of the Nile or African lily, need only be divided every four years – immediately after flowering ends – and their large fleshy roots separate easily. Plant in a good well-drained soil which includes a lot of compost and a cupful of bone phosphate.

Alstroemeria

Although the old-fashioned *A. aurantica*, the orange variety with a touch of carmine known as the Peruvian lily, is well worth having in your garden, today's range of *Ligtu* hybrids – pink, salmon, flame and

cream – is a must. They last well in water and are easy to grow.

Happiest in a rather sandy soil, alstroemeria enjoy some protection from the hot afternoon sun but with as bright a light as possible. They should always be planted slightly deeper than they were in the bag in which you bought them. They are slow to spread initially and hate being disturbed, but have patience and after the first few seasons you will be rewarded with large clumps of free-flowering beauties.

Physostegia

The obedience plant, so known because you can twist and turn the flowers on their stems and they will stay facing the direction in which you set them, provides many 60 cm-tall sturdy spikes bearing numbers of tubular mauve flowers in late summer. They are long-lasting in water.

Solidago canadensis

Ideal for late summer and autumn display, the Golden rod with its panicles of golden yellow flowers is valuable for border and vase alike. Many new varieties are available and there are 60 cm-tall varieties, as well as some that grow well over a metre.

Thalictrum aquilegifolum

A 90 cm tall shade-loving perennial, with dainty maidenhair-like foliage, it produces panicles of misty mauve flowers in late summer. It needs moisture constantly and enjoys a deep well-composted soil.

Bergenia megasea

For many years known as saxifrage, bergenia, which has spikes of lovely pink flowers rising from circles of attractive large leathery leaves, is a welcome addition to the winter scene. Happy in a light but shaded position, it is extremely easy to grow and makes a fine vase flower.

Gerbera jamesonii

Our indigenous Barberton Daisy has been transformed by the hybridizers and it is now possible to acquire a whole range of both single and double flowers in colours ranging from white and lime to pale pink and strong orange-red. Well-drained soil is their most important requirement and once planted they should be left undisturbed until their condition is obviously deteriorating. Separate in spring or early summer.

Kniphofia uvaria

Another indigenous perennial, the showy red hot poker, deserves a place in every arranger's garden. There are about 70 species in tropical Africa, and they can be found

growing as far north as Ethiopia. Their stately fiery torches are excellent for large arrangements and today even yellow and pink varieties are seen.

The striking flame coloured flowers show up best if planted in the border with a background of shrubbery and are most striking when grown in bold clumps. They flower in late autumn and in summer.

In areas of extreme frost it is best to lift your pokers for replanting the following spring. Propagation is by division. They enjoy a well drained soil in a sunny position.

Monarda didyma

With its charming ribbon-like flowers in purple, pink and red borne on 60 cm stems, bergamot is a lovely hardy perennial for the border, thriving in full sun or light shade. With clumps developing rapidly if given good soil and regular watering, it is worth separating these plants every two years.

Phlox paniculata

With their showy large round heads of bright flowers in a great variety of colours, the phlox is, not surprisingly, one of the most popular of hardy perennials. Suitable for full sun or dappled shade they need to be cut back in order to bush successfully.

The following list is of perennials suitable for both garden and vase which are generally fairly easily available in most parts of South Africa:

Tall and dainty Thalictrum, an indigenous perennial, is a joy in shade areas, having both beautiful maidenhair foliage and soft lilac blue flowers. Here it stands high above the neighbouring impatiens.

The silver-grey leaves, unusual blue flowers, and fragrance make lavender an important plant for garden and vase.

GERANIUMS

The pride of windowboxes from Grahamstown to Guinea, from Montevideo to Minsk, the simple little Cape flower, the geranium, is one of the world's best-loved plants.

Probably no plant is more widely used for providing colour in the home than the geranium and strangely enough this charming indigenous plant is most widely known and grown in Europe and America, where their sales increase by leaps and bounds every year.

As a result of the work done by hybridizers, mainly in West Germany, there are now new self-branching varieties, some which produce flowers more resistant to thunderstorms and disease, plants that are bushier and even some which are short-growing and ideally suited for the flat-dweller's balcony.

There was a time when geraniums grew mainly in orangey-red colours and pinks, but today the variety of colours and bi-colours is remarkable. They range from white to mixtures of red and white, purples and pinks, clear reds and carmines – the colours and combinations of colours are virtually endless.

Among the geranium's many assets is its easy cultivation – blooming successfully either in full sun, even in the hottest spots, or in light shade in a well-drained soil.

For geraniums really to succeed, monthly feeding is important and this should be given in either granular or liquid form. Although geraniums will survive neglect, it is amazing how they thrive with just a little extra tender loving care.

Geraniums need a fairly well-drained soil, they don't enjoy soggy ground, but in spite of this they should never be allowed to dry out. Some humus in the soil is an advantage.

Geraniums need little attention other than the occasional pinching back to encourage a bushy habit and masses of flowers. Cut back the plant when it becomes woody and you will soon be rewarded with lovely new growth.

Free-flowering geraniums provide a wonderful source of material for the vase for most of the year, on their own or in mixed arrangements.

Geraniums today come in a wide range of colours and bi-colours from white to vibrant reddish-purple, but the red and pink trailing ivy-leafed varieties remain popular.

The following are typical border perennials found in South African gardens and which have flowers, foliage or both suitable for flower arranging.

Botanical and common names	Height in cms	Leaves	Flowers	Aspect	Hardiness rating	Evergreen or die down	Comments
Acanthus mollis Wild Rhubarb	100	large, glossy, dark green indented	tall spikes of white and lilac	semi-shade	H	E	good accent plant
Agapanthus praecox minimus – large	100	broad, strap-like	light blue to dark blue and white, rounded umbels	sun or semi-shade	H	E	forms compact clumps, ideal under trees
Agapanthus praecox minimus – dwarf	50	narrow, strap-like	light blue to dark blue and white umbels	sun or semi-shade	H	E	forms compact clumps, ideal under trees
Alstroemeria aurantiaca Peruvian lily	60		trumpet flowers green-red, pink, pink, red, salmon	semi-shade	H	E	lovely in light shade, beautiful cut flower. Divide autumn, sow seed in spring
Alyssum saxatile 'Gold Dust'	25	grey-green	golden yellow	sun	H	E	attractive ground cover perfect for rockeries
Anchusa italica Forget-me-not	100	furry, grey-green	panicles of gentian blue	sun	H	E	ideal for arranging lovely in border
Anemone japonica Japanese anemone	60	mid-green, three-pointed maple-like	white, pink, saucer-shaped single and rose double	semi-shade	H	E	autumn flowering, fibrous rooted, grow best when feet in shade, heads in sun
Aquilegia alpinus 'Hensol's harebell' or Blue columbine	25	grey-green maidenhair-like	dark blue with short spurred bonnets	shade	H	E	attractive blue, unusual addition to garden and vase
Aquilegia vulgaris Columbine	60	grey-green maidenhair-like	long spurred bonnets, lovely pastel shades	semi-shade	H	D	flower for long period in summer if grown in bright shade where flowers don't burn
Armeria formosa Thrift	50	thin grass-like	pink glabose head on wiry stems	sun	H	E	hummock forming
Aster novi-belgii Michaelmas daisy	40	slender, pointed	spires of pink, blue, white, lavender small daisy-like blooms	sun	H	D	very accommodating and free flowering in various heights. Divide every 3 years
Aster alpinus	10	slender, grey-green	fluffy heads of misty blue	sun	H	E	prefers sun

Botanical and common names	Height in cms	Leaves	Flowers	Aspect	Hardiness rating	Evergreen or die down	Comments
Astilbe japonica Goat's Beard	70	palmately divided. Attractive leaves	white, pink and red feathery plumes	semi-shade	H	–	ideal surrounding water gardens and in shady borders in dry areas. Takes more sun in humid areas. Mixes well with irises, amaranthus and Japanese anemones
Bergenia cordifolia	25	large, glossy, leathery, attractive for arranging	heads of lilac-rose bells	sun or semi-shade	H	E	good cut flower. flowers late winter/early spring
Calliopsis lanceolata Coreopsis	25	mid-green pointed	bright yellow, red centre	sun	H	E	tough and drought resistant
Campanula glomerata Clustered bell flower		ovate and toothed	dense heads of erect purple bells	sun	H	D	needs good drainage
Canna indica gigantea Canna	50 to 150	broad, attractive with colours from light green to brown/purple plus striped and spotted forms	yellow, red, pink, orange	sun	SH	E	greedy feeder, needs deep rich soil plus ample water to thrive, divide every two years in spring, may be used as cut flower but limited life. Fine for floating bowls
Centaurea candidissima Dusty miller	30	silver, deeply lobed	yellow, daisy-like	sun	H	E	beautiful foliage for arrangements
Centaurea macrocephala	100	rough, light green	golden yellow thistles	sun	H	E	long-lasting cut flowers
Chrysanthemum maximum Shasta daisy	50	toothed, dark green	single or double white daisies	sun	H	E	useful cut flower, free-flowering. Divide every three years
Cineraria maritima	30	silvery, white felted	yellow daisies	sun	H	E	need good drainage
Delphinium 'Pacific Giant'	45 to 180	attractive divided leaves	blue, mauve, lilac, white, pink	sun	H	–	tall, it needs support, flowers in summer and if cut back again in autumn
Dianthus chinensis Carnation	45 to 75	narrow, small, curling silver grey	fragrant white red, pink, apricot, yellow, salmon	sun	H	E	needs good drainage, sandy soil, add little lime to soil, flowers well September to December but continuously until April

Botanical and common names	Height in cms	Leaves	Flowers	Aspect	Hardiness rating	Evergreen or die down	Comments
Dierama pendula Harebell	45 to 60	broad, strap-like, grassy leaves in clumps	slender stemmed lilac/pink to mauve, bell-like flowers	semi-shade	SH	E	ideal for water gardens, feed well with compost
Echinacea purpurea Pink rudbeckia	80	rough, slightly toothed	purple daisies with raised golden cone	sun	–	–	tough, strikingly attractive plant totally dormant in winter
Echinops ritro Globe thistle	100	hairy, grey green	globular, steel blue	sun	H	–	cut back in winter
Erigeron speciosus	30	mid-green	pink or mauve, many petalled, daisy-like	sun	H	E	cut back after flowering
Felicia amelloides Kingfisher daisy	30	rounded green	unusual king-fisher blue small daisies with bright yellow centres	sun	SH	E	bushy habit, extremely flori-ferous – but needs to be dead-headed regularly to keep neat and attractive
Gaillardia aristata Blanket flower	60 to 75	pointed dull green	long flowering through late summer into autumn and on into winter	sun or light shade	H	E	drought resistant but enjoys deep, rich soil and is a gross feeder – cutting promotes new growth
Gaura lindheimeri	50	long slender	dainty pink and white sprays on bush which appears to be covered with butter-flies	sun	SH	E	drought resistant
Geranium pratense ground cover or Carpet geranium	50	deeply divided mid-green	violet blue, crimson veined	semi-shade	H	E	spring flowering divide in autumn needs good drainage
Gerbera jamesonii Barberton daisy	30 to 60	deeply divided attractive foliage	now hybridized produces large range of colours from white through yellows to varied reds and oranges, flame and pinks	sun	H	E	excellent cut, needs good drainage. Do not divide too often, hates being disturbed
Geum chiloense	25	mid-green serrated	scarlet or yellow double	semi-shade	H	E	need to be able to spread for good display well drained soil flowers spring/summer

Botanical and common names	Height in cms	Leaves	Flowers	Aspect	Hardiness rating	Evergreen or die down	Comments
Helianthemum	25	small grey elliptic	pinks, reds, yellows	sun	SH	–	neat shrubby species related to rock rose, likes to ramble, flowers late spring. Trim after flowering to induce more flowers
Heliotrope 'Cherry pie'	25	dark green, finely wrinkled	fragrant, deep violet clusters	semi-shade	T		flowers fade quickly. Fast growing
Hemerocallis Day Lily	25 to 100	arching strap-like	trumpet shaped many coloured – oranges, yellows, pinks, reds, wines, bronzes	semi-shade	H	E	easy multiply to form large clumps flower spring to autumn
Heuchera sanguinea Coral bells	25	dark green heart shaped	tiny coral bells on slender stems	semi-shade	H	–	needs well drained soil
Hosta Plantain lily	40 to 60	foliage plant with beautiful broad leaves from light to dark green and variegated, ex-cellent for ar-rangements	white or blue white bell like flowers	shade	H	E	excellent for bog gardens or edge of streams
Iberis sempervirens Candytuft	20	small dark green	dense glistening white heads	sun	H	–	compact bush ideal for poor soil free flowering
Impatiens sultanii Busy Lizzy	20 to 45	fleshy mid green	double pink and purple but mainly simple single flower white, pink, red laven-der	shade	T	E	ideal shade plant flowers from spring until winter
Impatiens 'New Guinea' Sunshine impatiens	45	beautiful glossy and multi-col-oured forms with bronze, pink, yellow and yellow green forms	simple flowers in great profusion ranging from white and pink to salmon and red, purple and orange	semi-shade	T	E	free flowering, must have be-tween 4 and 6 hours sun for best leaf and flower colours
Incarvillea delavayi	60	handsome fern-like leaves	striking, large rose-coloured gloxinia-like flowers	semi-shade	T	–	sheltered position or lifted in cold places. Shows up well against other perennials, give rich, deep soil with lots of com-post, but which is well drained

Botanical and common names	Height in cms	Leaves	Flowers	Aspect	Hardiness rating	Evergreen or die down	Comments
Kniphofia aloibes Red hot poker	60	strap-like leaves	'poker' consists of many small tubular flowers in dense clusters which open orange, fade to yellow. Other colour forms range from tall creamy white to a dwarf pure yellow or orange	sun	SH	E	there are two types – summer and winter flowering, need well composted soil, should be well watered in spring – otherwise drought resistant, divide occasionally in spring
Liatris pycnostachya	90 to 150	tapering, dark green and glossy	unusual flower spikes with lovely shades of rosey-purple, flowers last well blooming throughout summer	sun	H	–	will grow in poor soil. Ideal plant for wild garden
Lobelia fulgens 'Queen Victoria'	100	dark plum coloured rosettes	brilliant scarlet spikes	semi-shade	SH	–	very showy, bog lover
Lobelia vedariense	100	lanceolate, dark green	purple spikes	semi-shade	SH	–	enjoys rich, moist soil
Lupinus polyphyllus Russell lupins	60+	attractive mid green digitate	many coloured with soft hues hybrids range from pale lemon to mauve	sun	H	–	prefer slightly acid soil, include peat moss in soil
Lychnis arkwrightii 'Vesuvius'	25	bronze-green	brilliant scarlet-orange	sun	H	E	needs support, flowers over long period if dead heads removed regularly fine for massing in beds
Lychnis viscaria 'Splendens'	25	thin and grass-like	carmine flowers in ovoid spike	semi-shade	H	E	dead-head plants regularly to prolong flowering period
Monarda didyma Bergamot	50	mid-green, slightly hairy	dense whorled heads of red or pink	sun	H	E	aromatic leaves spreads fairly rapidly, summer flowering, cut back in winter, divide regularly
Oxypetalum caeruleum	45	green-grey arrowhead	velvety electric blue starry	sun	T	E	shrubby, semi-climbing, flowers throughout summer

Botanical and common names	Height in cms	Leaves	Flowers	Aspect	Hardiness rating	Evergreen or die down	Comments
Paeonia officinalis Peony	60	attractive shiny dark green leaves	huge ball-like flowers in shades of pink, red, lemon and white	semi-shade	H	D	tuberous rooted, need cool moist rich soil, semi-shade or morning sun, compost soil well and feed regularly
Pelargonium hortorum Geranium	45	rounded, slightly hairy leaves, distinct dark zonal markings	great variety of colours from white, pink, salmon to red and bi-colours	sun	H	E	sandy, well drained soil, do not overwater, grow in open in pots, containers and window boxes, pinch to encourage bushi-ness
Pelargonium peltatum Trailing geranium	40	thick, shiny ivy-like leaves	great variety flowers, from white, pink, red, mauve and bi-colours	sun	SH	E	need, sandy, well drained soil, do not overwater. Ideal for con-tainers, window boxes, terraces, baskets, rockeries
Perlargonium domesticum Regal pelargonium	45	rough serrated	large butterfly-like flower in striking, plain and bi-colours from white and pink, to red, purple almost black	sun	H	E	sandy, well-drained soil, best in open ground, cut back and pinch new growth for bushiness
Penstemon heterophyllus Blue penstemon	40	grey, green, slender	spikes of deep blue flushed pink	sun	H	–	needs good drainage
Phlox paniculata Perennial phlox	50	mid green, lanceolate	dense ovoid panicles, white to rose shades, reds and purples	sun	H	–	require lots of water before and after flowering, cut down after flowering
Physostegia virginiana Obedience plant	40	mid-green sharply toothed	white or lavender spikes	semi-shade	H	E	good cut flower, requires copious watering, divide late autumn
Platycodon grandiflorus Balloon flower	40	broadly ovate, glaucous	balloon-like buds form saucer-shaped flowers	sun	H	–	dormant in winter
Polemonium caeruleum Jacob's ladder	50	forms mounds of feathery apple green leaves	racemes of blue saucer-shaped blooms	semi-shade	H	E	needs partly shaded position and moist soil, seeds itself when happy
Potentilla hirta pedata 'Cinquefoil'	30	dark green, digitate	bright yellow, saucer-shaped	sun	H	E	bushy habit

Botanical and common names	Height in cms	Leaves	Flowers	Aspect	Hardiness rating	Evergreen or die down	Comments
Primula polyanthus	20	rosette of green leaves	small primrose-shaped blooms in many brilliant colours	semi-shade	H	D	enjoys dappled shade, moist conditions
Prunella webbiana	25	mid-green, ovate	compact rosy spikes	sun or semi-shade	H	–	spreading habit good for cutting
Scabiosa caucasia	60		pincushion-like flowers on slender stems blooms through summer and autumn – white, light blue, dark blue, deep purple	sun	H	E	light well-drained soil essential
Solidago 'Baby gold', Golden rod	25	lanceolate, mid-green	golden-yellow plumes	sun	H	E	rounded bushy plant, good cut flower
Statice latifolium	50	rosette of downy leaves	dainty lavender blue panicles	sun	H	–	needs open sunny position, good cut flower
Statice perezzi	50	large flat leaves	panicles of violet blue	sun	H	–	flowers dry well
Stokesia cyanea Stoke's aster	25	lanceolate, mid green	large, showy blue asters	sun	H	–	need well-drained soil, dormant in winter
Teucrium chamaedrys Germander	20	grey-green, ovate	pinky-mauve flower spikes	sun	H	–	sub-shrub
Thalictrum aquilegifolium hybridum	90	dainty maiden-hair fern-like leaves	fine, delicate sprays of white/mauve flowers	shade	H	–	thrives in deep well-composted soil with moisture at all times
Tradescantia virginiana Spiderwort	30	dull green, pointed straps	terminal umbels of purple-blue	sun or semi-shade	H	E	
Verbena peruviana	30	fine, dark green leaves	cluster flowers white, red, pink, purple for many months from spring to winter	sun	H	–	ideal for rockeries, thrives in hot dry conditions
Veronica longifolia	100	deep green toothed	purple-blue terminal racemes	sun	H	E	cut down after flowering
Veronica spicata 'Rosea'	25	mid-green, oblong, toothed	pink, terminal racemes	sun or semi-shade	H	E	
Vinca rosea Periwinkle		green or variegated cream and green 'strings' of oval leaves excellent for foliage flower arrangements	small blue	semi-shade	H	E	excellent ground-cover, spreads rapidly

Botanical and common names	Height in cms	Leaves	Flowers	Aspect	Hardiness rating	Evergreen or die down	Comments
Viola hederacea Australian violet	15	light green, rounded leaves	small white flowers with mauve centre, blooms all year round	semi-shade	H	E	forms dense groundcover, spreads rapidly if grown in deep, cool soil, lovely for mini-arrangements
Viola odorata English violet	20	shiny, heart-shaped dark green leaves	fragrant flowers pink, lilac, purple	semi-shade	H	E	thrives in good soil, mulch regularly with compost
Zantedeschia aethiopica White arum	100	large glossy, green arrow-shaped, broad leaves	large white funnel-shaped spathes – a green-tipped variety known as green arum, also excellent for garden and vase	semi-shade	H	E	must be well-watered. Excellent for arrangements, flowers for long spell
Zantedeschia pentlandii Golden arum	75	handsome green leaves but also a spotted variety, Z. jucunda	lovely deep yellow funnel-shaped spathes	sun	H	D	dormant in winter, puts on brilliant show in summer, flowers last up to two weeks in vase
Zantedeschia rehmannii Pink arum	35	slender leaves tapering at tips	blooms rarely larger than 10 cm vary in colour from palest pink to rose and even a deep wine red	semi-shade	H	D	flowers in November, dormant in winter

E   Evergreen
D   Deciduous
H   Hardy
SH Semi-hardy
T   Tender

VII *Colour it bold*

Colour it bright, colour it bold, colour it green, gold yellow, white, blue or red. Nature has given the gardener the opportunity to work on a large canvas with all the colours imaginable, plus a thousand textures.

There is hardly a colour, if any, that is not included in the floral spectrum, and in your garden and flower arrangements it is possible to work with some colours that even the artist would find it hard to get away with. Who, for instance, would accept a green flower in a painting, yet in the garden you will find quite a few and they are a delight in interior designs.

When planting your garden be bold and where possible mass flowers of one colour together. They show up far better and look far less fussy used in large groups. Together they attract the eye – dotted about they worry it.

To save you the trouble of working out your own colour charts you will find columns of plants listed under individual colour headings at the end of this chapter. These lists are by no means exhaustive and you will find there are many, many more plants to work with as your garden develops. I aim only to give you a good basis on which to work.

White One of the most useful colours in any garden is white and the number of both large and small white flowers on offer is vast, and many are ideal for interior decoration.

The beauty of white is that it gives you two gardens for the price of one – one for day and another for night. There is nothing to match the ethereal loveliness of a white garden by moonlight, when banks of 'Iceberg' roses seem to almost sparkle and white nicotiana to glow, scenting the evening with a heady perfume.

White is also an extremely useful colour for the vase, either by itself or in mixed ar-

First flower to scent the garden at the end of winter is the delightful Chinese jasmine, which forms a froth of white from July into August. Here it is used in an opulent single flower arrangement, with its pink buds and white flowers showing up magnificently against the silver vase and christening mug.

rangements. For height in the vase there are a number of choices, such as agapanthus, cleomes, wild rhubarb (*Acanthus mollis*), Canterbury bells, dahlias and delphiniums, larkspurs, Mont Blanc (*Lavatera trimestris*) and lilies, with the fragrant St Joseph a must for any garden.

Small white blooms include those lovely little white border plants such as viola and verbena, alyssum and pansy. Between these

Poinsettias provide splashes of bright red in the landscape during late autumn-winter when there is little colour in the garden. With their long stems they are excellent for large arrangements but just a few flowers on short stems may be used in smaller arrangements.

two extremes is an enormous range of plants from fairly low-growing petunias to taller nikkis and Japanese anemones.

WHITE CREEPERS

Creepers are a wonderful source of white flowers and a great many of these are excellent for use in the home, either by themselves or in mass arrangements.

Three great favourites are jasmines – Star jasmine (*Trachelospermum jasminoides*), Chinese jasmine (*Jasminum polyanthum*) and Chilean jasmine (*Mandevilla suaveolens*). Their beautiful fragrance makes them ideal candidates for the vase.

Particularly desirable is that immaculate creeper, the Star jasmine, with its shiny dark leaves an excellent foil for the galaxies of tiny white star-like flowers, like a Milky Way against the night sky. Rugged and capable of enduring a fair amount of frost, it will grow in virtually any position, even in shade, and it will creep or trail and may even be trimmed into a shrub.

One of the most fragrant of creepers and among the first to herald spring is the Chinese jasmine with its froth of flowers. With dainty cerise buds which open into pure white flowers, the overall mass of bloom often gives a rosy pink effect. It is stunning alone in a vase, but its long trailing stems topped by heavy panicles of flowers are also wonderful fillers in large arrangements such as those suitable for a church.

Both these jasmines grow well in large containers, and are thus ideal for flat balconies and townhouse patios.

Mandevilla grows easily from seed and has a fabulous lily-like fragrance – particularly at night. Flowering for many months from October until late summer, it is a fast and vigorous grower, billowing over walls and very attractive when grown up a trellis. It is tough and needs little attention other than to be tidied up during winter.

As picked flowers the jasmines are easily arranged and particularly suitable for dinner table arrangements – mandevilla and Star jasmine are excellent vase companions, complementing one another and virtually arranging themselves. Little special treatment is necessary except to pop the ends of their milky stems into boiling water for a few minutes to seal them.

In South Africa all-white arrangements are often considered as being suitable only for funerals, weddings or large church decorations. In fact they are ideal for indoors as they blend with any colour scheme and give a welcome cooling appearance in our hot climate.

Two beautiful white creepers (above) for the garden, which are particularly suitable for patios and small gardens are Chilean jasmine (*Mandevilla suaveolens*) and the Star jasmine (*Trachelospermum jasminoides*). Both are excellent in small arrangements and in the picture are combined to produce a round arrangement.

Pink Next to white, the biggest flower colour range is pink. This is just as well, for pink is probably the most popular colour for interior decorating and so masses of cut flowers in this shade are constantly in demand.

Probably one of the finest sources of pink for the vase is the rose family, for it covers the full range from the palest of pinks ('Porcelain') to salmon ('Elizabeth of Glamis') and the deepest of cyclamen pinks ('Electron'), with an incredible variety of shades in between.

Another source of beautiful pinks are the camellias, azaleas, geraniums and a great variety of blossoms, from peach and plum to crab-apple. Annuals, too, are a wonderful source of pink with petunias providing beauties such as 'Pink Satin' and 'Apple Blossom'. For other lovely pinks try nicotiana (pink and rose) and *Lavatera trimestris*, which has a rather luminous quality.

Blue Gardeners often complain of a lack of blue, yet there are many beautiful blues available – with hydrangeas being a striking source in high summer. Three indigenous plants provide some of the loveliest shades of blue – our sky-blue plumbago (*P. capensis*) agapanthus and the little Felicia.

Incidentally, the small Japanese plumbago is well worth growing for its very special deep blue colour.

Another not to be overlooked source of blue is that willing little charmer, the Forget-me-not (*Myosotis alpestris*). Grown in compost-rich soil in a lightly shaded position, this little beauty flowers in winter and spring. If it is kept well watered it will flourish for you, even sowing itself about the garden.

Not as well-known but boasting a particularly beautiful blue is the aquilegia, a most attractive plant, but strangely, never included in the normal Columbine mixtures one finds in nurseries – it needs to be sought out.

A shrub offering two tones of blue is the unusual Oxford and Cambridge bush (*Clerodendron ugandense*), with its clusters of delicate little butterfly flowers. It blooms for many months of the year but is at its best in autumn – a time when flowers are often hard to find, which makes it very valuable for the flower arranger.

Lasting up to three days in the vase it is delightful in mixed arrangements or in vases with pink or yellow roses. The only treatment it needs for use indoors is to have its stems seared in boiling water for a few moments.

Not at all fussy about its soil, the Oxford and Cambridge bush soon grows into a

LAVATERA TRIMESTRIS

Pink in profusion is provided by *Lavatera trimestris*, one of the finest annuals to have appeared on the gardening scene in many years.

This glistening pink, rather bushy member of the hollyhock family caused the biggest sensation of the century in seed circles in the late 1970s when it was awarded the Silver Cup – the highest award ever given an annual plant in an international flower competition.

Growing to close on a metre tall, the plant has an excellent bushy habit and should be planted at least 65 to 75 cm apart. They are such fine looking subjects – pyramids of colour, covered in 8 cm wide frilly flowers. They may be used either as striking groups, towards the back of an herbaceous border or planted in one breathtaking bed of shiny pink which lasts from six to eight weeks.

Lavatera plants are also most striking when interplanted with either roses, 'Pacific Giant' delphiniums or dahlias.

Like petunias, lavatera are most successful when grown during the dry winter months but will also do well in the summer rainfall region if planted late so that they flower towards the end of the rainy season. They should be planted in well composted soil containing a light sprinkling of 2:3:2 fertilizer.

If planted early the seedlings may have damping off problems and may at first need regular treatments with a fungicide such as Fungisprey or Benlate.

For indoor arrangements lavateras need no treatment at all, other than regular topping up of water in the vase. They are ideal for compact table centre-pieces, using short 10 cm to 15 cm branchlets, or for medium height displays and last well in the vase with buds opening over a period of about five days. Although they may be used in mixed bowls their own green leaves are sufficient to make them striking single flower arrangements.

PLUMBAGO

So common that people hardly notice it any longer, our indigenous *Plumbago capensis*, with its multitude of simple sky-blue, phlox-like blooms, is a must for any garden and a wonderful source of flowers for the vase.

Known to be Cecil John Rhodes' favourite flower this lovely shrub grows wild throughout Southern Africa from the Cape to the Matopas.

A rambling evergreen with a tendency to scramble into trees if given the chance, plumbago normally grows to about 2 m tall and just as wide. It flowers intermittently in the spring and profusely for a long period during the summer and autumn. The blooms are borne in clusters on the ends of branches.

Easy to grow, plumbago is useful as a dense screener, it looks superb tumbling down a bank or it may be trimmed into an excellent hedge. Keep an eye on plumbago grown as a shrub or it may get out of control; it is a good idea to cut it back severely each winter.

Drought resistant and hardy to frost, it is a most adaptable plant and will even grow in the shade, although it flowers far better in full sunlight. In addition to the blue there is also a white variety, while southern Asia is home to a pink plumbago.

As a vase flower, plumbago is ideal for simple arrangements. It needs no special treatment other than the removal of the sticky dead flowers which sometimes cling to the stems. It lasts for three days in the vase and if the weather is not too hot it may last even longer.

The Cape's drought resistant plumbago is a must for South African gardens, offering arrangers a very special sky blue for their vases. It is used to excellent effect in two very different arrangements.

rather lanky untidy bush, unless cut back severely each winter to keep its shape. After its flowers have passed, it produces attractive yellow berries which may also be used for arrangements if the birds don't beat you to the picking.

Blue is very much a day colour – at night blue flowers are inclined to be lost in the gloom. An exception to this is blue salvia. Its spikes stand out clearly, particularly if contrasted with something like gypsophila.

The difficulty of blue is to give it life in the vase and it is here that the wall background is so important. Suitable colours to contrast with blue are lime green, white and particularly pale yellow. Two of the loveliest deep blue flowers, delphiniums and cornflowers, look exceedingly attractive against this colour.

Although the colour of the container can also give a blue arrangement a lift, and here white vases play an important role, the design itself will be improved by the inclusion of bright touches of red and a lot of white and yellow blooms.

Green Yellow, red, orange and purple are relatively easy colours to come by in the garden but one must go out of one's way to collect green flowers. There are not a great number of these but they are very rewarding and certainly well worth having in your arranger's armoury.

Bells of Ireland (*Molucella laevis*) is one of the most popular of the green flowers, but do not overlook the green arum, the lime green nikki, the appropriately named 'Envy' zinnia and, of course, the head of the hydrangea which, after holding its colour for summer, slowly changes first through pink to green in autumn.

Although not strictly a flower, the spiky flower ball of the agapanthus after the flowers and seed heads have been removed, makes a fascinating green 'flower' which is a wonderful addition to any arrangement. These heads may also be dried and used very effectively in autumn arrangements.

Yellow Yellow is one of the safest colours to use in arrangements, especially for people in hospital as it is a cheery colour and brightens any room. It is always wise to have a variety of yellow flowers in the garden and this is not difficult for there is a wide variety of shadings from the green-yellow of 'Pineapple Crush' marigolds to the pale lemon yellow of the 'Lemon Queen' Marguerite, not forgetting the brightness of a buttercup.

Almost the symbol of yellow flowers is the sunflower which in another age was one of the most popular cut flowers for the vase,

as the paintings of Van Gogh and other artists indicate, but today, sadly, they are rarely seen.

Gardeners are inclined to think of sunflowers in terms of the 2 m tall varieties which grow in rows as far as the eye can see on Transvaal and Free State farms, but in fact there are many decorative varieties not nearly so tall, and which, given a good soil, grow very easily from seed.

Finding these seeds in South Africa is very difficult as none of the seed companies have them available. My enquiries to firms received a 'There's no demand' reply, which is most unfortunate for sunflowers are really worthwhile additions to the garden. Arrangers should start pestering seed companies to return them to the rack.

It is sometimes possible to get seeds from friends but if this fails then the best is to order from overseas catalogues. Varieties worth trying are *Helianthus decapetalis* (Loddon Gold), about 1,2 m; *H.* 'Californian Double Giants', 1,25 m; *H. multiflorus*, double and single reds, bronze and yellow, 0,30 m to 1,5 m and *H.* 'Teddy Bear', large double round puff ball flower, 0,90 m.

Sunflowers produce two crops for the gardener growing for the vase: the large initial flower cut from each plant will last for a long time, even weeks, in the vase and is followed by a multitude of smaller florets which develop in the leaf axils of the plants.

Orange Another bright and cheery colour is orange, but in the vase it is not quite as easy on the eye as it is when in the garden. Although a bold arrangement of solid orange can be effective in the right setting it may be rather over-powering. Orange is a colour which usually succeeds best in mixed arrangements. It is a good contrast colour especially with blue, particularly dark blue delphiniums, and yellow. In the garden a lovely combination is the dark blue lobelia and the small 'Lemon Drop' marigolds.

Red Brighter but even more difficult in the vase are red flowers, certainly as a single colour, but they are excellent for giving an arrangement a lift, with bright highlights adding lightness and gaiety to an otherwise ordinary design.

Oddly, red is not a night colour and one must be very careful of using it in arrangements which will depend to a large extent on artificial light. Red is the sign of danger so treat it as such; be very wary of it in your interiors.

Red roses are one of the exceptions. A classic presentation is the simple glass vase, preferably a cylinder, holding a dozen red roses but even these are enhanced by a few

PETUNIAS

Petunias are very underrated as a cut flower. They are rarely seen in arrangements yet they make a lovely show. Their range of colours is large and they make a fine display in containers on patios and at poolsides, massed in the garden, hanging in baskets and in the vase.

Petunias are one of the most successful of bedding plants in dry areas and during dry seasons, therefore in the Cape they generally do far better in summer, while in the Transvaal they thrive during the dry and sunny winter months.

Well drained soil is ideal for petunias, par-

Petunias offer a wonderful range of colour for the garden.

ticularly in the damper months. If it is your intention to grow petunias in containers, ensure that there is a good layer of river sand at the bottom to allow excess water to drain away rapidly.

Petunias are frail plants, so do take care when picking them. Other than this they are undemanding flowers. Once in the vase they last for many days and continue to open over a period, particularly if the water is changed regularly.

sprays of gypsophila to soften the effect.

It is at Christmas time that red comes into its own and somehow always looks right. Bright carnations, roses and hibiscus are all available at this time, and the use of some of the flowers for Christmas decorations will be discussed later.

All-green arrangements are quite a modern vase form in the West and can be most attractive. They will be discussed in the chapter on foliage, together with those other popular modern colour choices – grey and silver.

DELICATE PLANTS FOR SMALL ARRANGEMENTS

Small arrangements are useful for areas such as bookcase shelves, small tables, dressing-table tops and breakfast trays, and there are a great variety of small colourful flowers particularly suited to these positions.

In spring there are small blooms aplenty, with miniature roses, violets and English daisies all readily available. You will be able to find suitable flowers during most months of the year, with nasturtiums, geraniums and plumbago, lavender, rosemary and abelia available at most times.

A flower which is particularly suitable for small arrangements is the petrea. This creeper, now available in both blue and white, produces many hundreds of flowers when mature. The spikes of the flowers are most attractive and will keep in a small vase for several days. See also the list at the end of the chapter.

Periwinkle is an extremely useful small groundcover choice, as is Ajuga, and both flowers and foliage are useful.

When it comes to foliage for small arrangements, one may use snippets of practically anything, but particularly suitable are the leaves of fern, conifer and asparagus varieties, material such as sprigs of abelia and nandina, the feathery leaves of columbine and, for a touch of silver grey, Lamb's ears (*Stachys*) or the foliage of herbs such as artemesia or santolina.

Some useful flowers for mini arrangements:

Abelia varieties
Ajuga reptans
Alyssum
Armeria
Blue Salvia
Columbine
Dianthus
English daisy (*Bellis perennis*)

Geum
Gypsophila
Hypericum 'Hidcote'
Lavender
Limonium latifolium
Miniature roses
Mock orange blossom
Periwinkle
Petrea varieties
Plumbago
Rosa 'Cecille Brunner'
Violet varieties

The following lists of various coloured flowers will help arrangers when planning colour schemes in their gardens:

BLUE

Agapanthus
Ageratum
Aster varieties
Balloon flower
Blue salvia
Blue lace flower
Caryopteris
Catmint (*Nepeta*)
Cineraria
Columbine
Cornflower
Delphinium
Eustoma
Felicia
Forget-me-not
Hyacinth
Hydrangea
Iris
Lisianthus russellianus
Lobelia
Muscari
Pansy
Petunia
Plectranthus
Plumbago
Queen Anne's Lace
Rosemary
Salvia
Scabious (*Scabiosa*)
Sweet pea
Vinca
Viola

BROWN (BRONZE)

Chrysanthemum
Day lily
Dombeya
Gaillardia
Holmskioldia
Iris
'Julias's' rose
Marigold
Melianthus major

Rudbeckia
Woodrose
Zinnia

GREEN

Agapanthus heads
Alstroemeria
Arums
Bells of Ireland
'Greensleeves' rose
Hydrangea var.
Liriodendron tulipifera
Nikki lime
Zinnia Envy

ORANGE

Alstroemeria
Calendula
Canna
Dahlia
Day lily
Gaillardia
Gladiolus
Iceland poppy
Leonotus leonorus
Lily
Marigold
Nasturtium
Nemesia
Pyracantha var. (berries)
Rose varieties
Strelitzia
Sunflower
Zinnia

MAUVE (Purple)

Ageratum
Alyssum
Aster var.
Candytuft
Canterbury bells
Dahlia
Delphinium
Foxglove
Geranium
Hydrangea
Iris
Larkspur
Lavender
Liatris
Limonium
Michaelmas daisy
Pelargonium
Penstemon
Petunia
Phlox
Plectranthus
Rose var.
Scabiosa
Statice
Sweet pea

Thalictrum
Veronica
Violet

PINK

Abelia 'Edward Goucher'
Ageratum
Armeria
Aster
Azalea
Barberton daisy
Bergenia
Blushing bride
Camellia
Canterbury bell
Carnation
Cherry
Chrysanthemum
Clarkia
Cleome
Cornflower
Cosmos
Crab apple
Daffodil
Dahlia
Daisy
Delphinium
Deutzia gracilis
Dianthus
Digitalis
Dombeya
Erica var.
Escallonia 'Apple blossom'
Flowering quince
Frangipani
Geranium
Gladiolus
Gypsophila
Hibiscus
Honeysuckle
Hyacinth
Hydrangea
Iceland poppy
Japanese anemone
Larkspur
Lavatera trimestris
Magnolia
Marguerite
Nerine
Nikki
Penstemon
Peony
Petunia
Phlox
Primula
Protea
Rose var.
Snapdragon
Spiraea
Stocks
Sweet pea
Tamarisk

SILVER OR GREY *(foliage)*

Artemesia
Dusty miller (*Senecio*)
Lamb's ear (*Stachys lanata*)
Lavender
Rue
Santolina

RED

Alstroemeria
Amaranthus
Astilbe
Azalea
Carnation
Cosmos
Crab-apple
Dahlia
Day lily
Dianthus
Flowering quince
Foxglove
Geranium
Gladiolus
Hydrangea
Kaffirboom
Nasturtium
Nikki
Pansy
Pelargonium
Peony
Petunia
Phlox
Red hot poker
Rose
Salvia
Snapdragon
Sweet pea
Tulip
Viola
Zinnia

WHITE

Achillea
Ageratum
Alyssum
Aster var.
Astilbe
Azalea
Camellia var.
Candytuft
Canterbury bell
Carnation
Choisya ternata
Cornflower
Chrysanthemum
Clarkia
Cleome
Cosmos
Crabtree
Daffodil
Dahlia

Daisy
Delphinium
Deutzia
Dianthus
Elderberry
Feverfew
Flowering quince
Gardenia
Geranium
Gladiolus
Gypsophila
Honeysuckle
Hyacinth
Hydrangea macrophilla
Hydrangea quercifolia
Hydrangea paniculata
Iris
Japanese anemone
Jasmine var.
Larkspur
Lavatera trimestris
Wild rhubarb (*Acanthus*)

YELLOW

Achillea
Arctotis
Calendula
Calliopsis
Canna
Chrysanthemum
Coreopsis
Daffodil
Dahlia
Day lily
Feverfew
Forsythia
Gaillardia
Gladiolus
Golden rod (*solidago*)
Helianthus
Iceland poppy
Iris
Jasmine
Kerria
Lily
Marguerite
Marigold
Nasturtium
Nemesia
Pansy
Petunia
Poppy
Red hot poker
Rose varieties
Rudbeckia
Snapdragon
Solidago
Sunflower
Tulip
Viola
Wild rhubarb (*Acanthus mollis*)
Zinnia

VIII   *Background bloomers*

Shrubs, trees and climbers may well be the background plants of the garden but they are also an area – often overlooked – capable of supplying a lot of cut flowers.

Plant a well-planned shrubbery including just one tree – a frangipani and three shrubs – hibiscus, flowering quince and plumbago – and you will virtually have something flowering in the garden all year round. Add to this a couple of good climbers, such as a bougainvillea, honeysuckle, virginia and an 'Iceberg' rose and there will be few of the fifty-two weeks in which you are without blooms or foliage of some kind.

Include a few good foliage plants, such as the Japanese sacred bamboo (*Nandina domestica*) and *Asparagus plumosa*, discussed in the next chapter, and you won't necessarily need a great deal more, particularly if you are living on a small plot.

In colder areas your choice is rather more restricted but with climber roses against a nice warm wall, a flowering quince (*Chaenomeles lagenaria*), a fire thorn (*Pyracantha angustifolia*) with its striking orange berries, some abelias and a plumbago, your needs will be fairly well provided for in the cooler months.

Cold climate gardeners often complain because they cannot grow bougainvillea and hibiscus, but to compensate they are blessed in being able to enjoy many plants that people in warmer climates are unable to grow. Among these are such beautiful shrubs as the rhododendron and forsythia. Another is that splendid photinia-like shrub, the *Pieris japonica*, which not only has lovely white, almost lily-of-the-valley-like flowers but bright red early leaf shoots, crowding the bush at the same time as the flowers. Flowering in early spring, its branches, tightly packed with lovely leaves and cascades of flowers, it needs little preparation for the vase other than to have stem ends hammered.

Train your eye to pick up all manner of flowering shrubs, trees and climbers which

A waterfall of golden banksias.

might be suitable for cutting for the vase – whether you are in the veld or in a friend's garden. You will find a great variety of material worth testing.

Who would think for instance that the dombeya, a tree often seen growing in the wild, is a wonderful source of fresh picked flowers when grown in the garden and that its delicate pink and white blooms are lovely when dried (see also chapter on Special Occasions).

Charming catkins for use as decoration are provided by the pussy willow (*Salix caprea*), while China's lovely Golden rain tree (*Koelreuteria paniculata*) produces most attractive bladder-like seed pods which change in colour from a greenish-yellow, through pink to brown.

Our indigenous Wild cotton ball (*Asclepias physocarpa*), with its puffy balloon-like pods, is something else you should seek out – and do collect seed when you find it for you are unlikely to be able to buy it anywhere. All these plants are ideal for floral decoration and the enthusiastic arranger will find there are masses of other wonderful indigenous varieties with striking seed heads which one can try planting in the garden.

Climbers – so easy to grow and a very useful source of additional cutting material, particularly for small garden enthusiasts

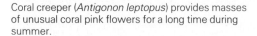
Coral creeper (*Antigonon leptopus*) provides masses of unusual coral pink flowers for a long time during summer.

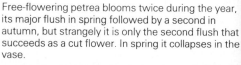
Free-flowering petrea blooms twice during the year, its major flush in spring followed by a second in autumn, but strangely it is only the second flush that succeeds as a cut flower. In spring it collapses in the vase.

where space for plants is limited – offer a tremendous number of attractive flowers. These range from the bougainvillea, whose bright bracts may be preserved, to coral creeper (*Antigonon leptopus*) and the fragrant *Stephanotis floribunda*.

The petrea, too, with its blue and white varieties, produces thousands of flowers in a season and is ideal for small arrangements. Use only the flower spikes, stripping off some of the florets at the bottom. The petrea has two major flowering periods – in spring and autumn – and oddly it is only the autumn blooms that one may use in arrangements. In spring they flop almost immediately.

Another extremely useful creeper for design material is the common honeysuckle (*Lonicera* varieties). Not only is there a choice of flower colours, including a bush form with red blooms, but there is also one with yellow-veined variegated leaves, which is most attractive and its lovely trailing stems are a delight in the vase.

White creepers are an excellent source of blooms, and rather strangely are generally better lasting than those of their more colourful cousins (see Chapter 7).

The Christmas rose, as the hydrangea is known in South Africa, is another wonderful source of blooms, especially during the summer holiday season when there is often very little else in the garden.

Delightful in arrangements, the variegated honeysuckle (*Lonicera japonica* 'Aureo-reticulata') is a must for the garden. Ensure that it grows in sun, however, or the netted green and gold leaves will turn green.

58

ROSES

One of the best and most popular sources of flowers in the world is the rose, which is after all a shrub, although one is inclined to overlook the fact.

There is an enormous variety of roses – either shrubs or climbers. Although no garden should be without some kind of rose, be it a normal HT, floribunda, standard or miniature, it is also well worth finding a space for one of the climbers. These offer many charming forms, from the trusses of banksia roses and charming single yellow 'Mermaids' to sparkling 'Icebergs' and great Hybrid Tea roses, such as 'Super Star' and 'Charlotte Armstrong'.

Year after year the rose retains its position as the world's favourite flower. Its beauty is undoubtedly its main attraction, but also in its favour is the fact that it is easy to grow, it is a prolific bloomer and many varieties offer fragrance as a bonus. For the hard-pressed housewife the rose is a wonderful asset. Just one in a vase makes a charming decoration, while a mass of blooms causes a sensation.

For anyone wishing to start a rose garden the best time is July/August, when nurseries get their supplies for the year and the choice is widest. Nor will you have long to wait for flowers, for within a matter of three months your bushes will be covered in blooms.

Most roses continue flowering on and off from October until frost cuts them back, while others bloom virtually non-stop and in warmer areas often continue happily until pruned in late July/August. The two main flushes of flowers, however, occur in October and January/February.

There are thousands of rose varieties and certainly in the Republic many hundreds of the better known are available. In addition growers are always introducing exciting new ones, so it is worth asking your local garden centre for their current rose list.

Still tops in the popularity stakes are the pinks, with 'Queen Elizabeth' well ahead of the field. This large bushed rose which produces masses of delicate pink blooms in a season is ideal for the back of a bed but must be given plenty of room.

Other extremely popular pinks are 'Sylvia' and 'Sonia', the latter being a florist's favourite because of its small full blooms which retain their salmon-pink colouring and hold well in the vase. The range of pinks available is impressive, but one of the most delicately-coloured and superb blooms for flower arranging is 'Porcelain', a medium-sized rose with a beautifully shaped bud.

Four roses that remain popular year in and year out: 'Iceberg' (below); 'Courvoisier' (top right); 'Satchmo' (centre); 'Pernille Poulsen' (bottom).

'Peace', with its large cream to golden yellow blooms tinged with rose remains a favourite, as do the reds – 'Mr Lincoln' a rich red on long stems and 'Oklahoma', so dark it is almost black.

When it comes to fragrance 'Duftwolke' ('Fragrant Cloud') is hard to beat. One bloom of this vermilion coloured charmer will perfume a room. Its other assets are the exquisitely shaped buds borne on long stiff stems – certainly worth having in any garden.

One of the loveliest roses for flower arranging and one with a very special hue is 'Antique Silk', which is the colour of raw silk but with a faint pink sheen. Its exquisite colour is enhanced by its excellent shape – an exceptional rose!

For anyone with the space in their garden a bush of 'Cecille Brunner', a dainty pink miniature which grows into a vast bush (2m × 2 m or more) with arching stems covered in clusters of mini double blooms – can hardly be left out. This very busy plant

'Freesia' roses were chosen to accompany this wedding picture on a Golden Wedding day.

Ever popular 'Peace' makes an excellent climbing rose.

'Duftwolke' ('Fragrant Cloud'), an excellent cut rose, is a delight in any room.

which flowers on and off throughout the summer, produces many hundreds and possibly thousands of flowers in a season.

When planting your rose bushes, use liberal amounts of compost and well-rotted manure in your beds – together with some general fertilizer such as SR 3:2:1 (28) – 45g per sq m of bed. Dig holes at least two or three times the size of the rose container. After removing the plastic bag place the plant in the hole so that the graft union is at the same level as the surrounding soil.

Once planted, firm down well and apply about 20 litres of water to each rose to settle the soil and remove air pockets. Sprinkle a handful of superphosphate around the plant before watering. Next add a mulch of well-rotted kraal manure around the plant but not against the stem.

For people living in flats with sunny balconies or those who have roof gardens, it is worth growing a few miniature roses in containers, for their blooms crowd the plants for many months and when picked make charming small arrangements. Particularly good varieties are: 'Amoretta', a white with a perfect bud; 'Guletta', a golden yellow; 'Eleanor', an attractive coral pink double; 'Ocarina', a double garnet-shaped rose of light vermilion blending to yellow and 'Rosmarin', a silvery rose with a scarlet centre. For those who have the space for a larger container, the free-flowering floribundas, such as 'Freesia', a fragrant strong yellow, and the glowing red 'Satchmo', are ideal plants for picking material.

When picking roses, whether blooms or buds, it is wise to cut them in the evening, split the stems, and place them in deep tepid water overnight. With a rose stripper remove the lower thorns and the leaves from stems, keeping only three to five leaves at the top, as this goes to make a better arrangement.

Another important factor when cutting roses is to prune as you pick, as this ensures more and better blooms later. To do this always cut above an eye or outward-facing leaf joint. This will ensure a better-shaped bush.

Cut roses will last from two to five days depending on the weather; it is wise to keep vases topped up with a little water all the time.

Roses blend beautifully with other flowers in mixed bowl arrangements. Here 'Sweet Repose' and 'Sonia' are seen with sweetpeas, ranunculus, pink daisies and pink honeysuckle in a fresh spring bowl.

Massed rose beds provide a wonderful display of colour and blooms picked for the vase are never missed. The pale pink rose on the left is 'Sylvia', the florists' favourite. The other roses from front to back are: the free-flowering yellow 'Freesia', the dark red 'Satchmo', and at the back the glorious pink 'Queen Elizabeth'.

61

All roses may be used with success in the vase but there are some with outstanding qualities – long-lasting, well-shaped buds, and with the exceptional colour and fragrance, which flower arrangers particularly appreciate. Among these are:

Name	Description
HYBRID TEA	
'American Heritage'	Cream to light yellow, contrasting with scarlet and vermilion in open flower. Vigorous, free-flowering.
'Antique Silk'	Extraordinary wild silk colour with blush sheen. Beautifully shaped small buds. Full of character.
'Bel Ange'	Soft pink blooms with darker reverse on long stems. Flowers continously.
'Black Pearl'	Dark red, almost black, pointed buds on long stems. Lasts well in water.
'Chicago Peace'	Enormous, full exhibition blooms. Pink with canary-yellow reverse and copper tones. Rigid stems.
'Duftwolke' ('Fragrant Cloud')	Extremely fragrant orange-vermilion with tangerine red. Exquisitely shaped buds opening to double flowers.
'Exciting'	Splendid cut flower loved by florists. Flame red, long pointed buds, long straight stems. Lasts well.
'Greensleeves'	Charming floribunda rose with good bud which opens pink then turns soft green. Dries well.
'Julia's Rose'	Excellent H.T. cut rose, with unusual beige/coffee coloured blooms.
'Love Story'	Brilliant coral red, gleaming silky petals, perfectly formed buds.

Name	Description
'Melina'	Lasting many days when cut. Scarlet red double blooms on rigid stems. Opens attractively.
'Montezuma'	Profuse bloomer. Scarlet orange large full blooms. Last well on plant and in vase.
'National Trust'	Vivid cardinal red blooms. Last well on plant and in vase. Elegant, scented.
'Oklahoma'	Highly scented black-red, with beautifully shaped, long-lasting blooms.
'Peace'	Large flowers, creamy pale gold-yellow with rose pink, borne on good stems.
'Porcelain'	Delicate pink, medium size. Beautifully-shaped bud.
'Prince Claus'	Orange-red firm urn-shaped fragrant rose. Vigorous grower.
'Red Success'	Well formed tight buds, brilliant red, double flowers. Popular with cut-flower trade.
'Rodin'	Free-flowering ruby red and white. Very decorative in vase. Long, pointed, exhibition form. Free flowering and robust.
'Sonia'	Florist's choice. Soft salmon pink. Full blooms retain colour.
'Super Star'	Ideal cut flower. Intense vermilion with full well-formed fragrant blooms. Lasts well in water.
'Tiffany'	Pink blended with gold. Both bud and bloom are graceful and elegant.
'Queen Elizabeth'	Superb and delicate pure pink rose on large bush. Long stems, profuse bloomer.

Name	Description
FLORIBUNDA	
'Fidelio'	Vivid scarlet, sweetly scented. Flowers in profusion. Long-lasting large blooms on long stiff stems.
'Freesia'	Strongly scented, bright yellow. Floriferous. Does not fade.
'Iceberg'	Probably flowers more than any other rose. White with blush tinge.
'Marina'	Luminous orange changing to salmon. Long-lasting blooms. Forms clusters of shapely buds.
'Tickled Pink'	Vigorous plant with long pointed buds. Porcelain rose with carmine reverse.
MINIATURE	
'Dwarf King'	Blood red, lovely shapely buds, open to rosette. Flowers throughout summer.
'Guletta'	Golden-yellow with quick-repeating flowering habit. Fairly large cup-shaped blooms.
'Ocarina'	A true miniature. Produces abundant charming, glowing salmon buds and blooms with yellow at base of reverse. Hold garnet shape for long time.
'Rosmarin'	Silvery rose with scarlet red centre. Double blooms throughout summer.

BOUGAINVILLEA

Brightest and most colourful of all the climbers seen in South Africa are the bougainvilleas, those bold beauties that race up tall trees, cascade over walls and enliven patio pots, delighting all who see them each summer.

Though many are the attempts that end on the compost heap, bougainvilleas do make beautiful arrangements. Even if it is a hit and miss affair preserving their blooms, you will find your successes are so spectacular as to make your efforts worthwhile.

The secret of success with these brilliant climbers is to pick only well matured flowers – those that have almost dried themselves on the plant. Picking any that have young florets is a complete waste of time.

For a fresh arrangement the most successful method is to use rather short stems, scraped at the ends and then left in water containing a tablespoon of vinegar for about 10 minutes before arranging.

There are a great many ways of drying bougainvillea ranging from baking it in an oven to covering it with silica gel. For the average person, however, who has not the time for too much fuss, one of the best methods is still to tie bunches together and hang upside down in a dark room, under the stairs or in a basement, away from draughts. One of the main advantages with this method is that once dried the flowers are all facing upwards in the arrangement.

Another successful method is to place cut stems of bougainvillea in trays in the oven. Pre-heat your oven to 160°C and switch off to avoid scorching. Leave the plants in the oven for two hours and then take out to cool. Unfortunately with this method you are limited as to the length of stem by the size of the oven. Should you need longer lengths, however, it is a fairly easy matter to wire or tape large flower clusters to sticks or pieces of split bamboo. The only preparation necessary before placing bougainvillea bracts in an oven is to remove all leaves and thorns from stems.

Bougainvilleas are ideal plants for hot dry areas, being most colourful in drought conditions. During normal years it is unnecessary to water bougainvilleas in the garden, and even those in tubs need only a little attention once a week. Too much water and food result in rich green growth and few flowers.

For greatest success with bougainvilleas, trim back after flowering and they will pro-

For small gardens where there are limits to the number of creepers you can grow, a bougainvillea should be a number one choice if only for the length of time it flowers. This white variety (*B. alba*) is a very strong grower.

The pink varieties appear to be the most successful bougainvilleas for dry arrangements.

duce even more profusely the following season.

Although they will not survive severe frost, some bougainvilleas can take a little or are not badly damaged by it. Some may even be grown in frosty gardens, such as in parts of the Free State, if given a cosy and protected corner against a warm wall which retains some of its heat overnight.

It has been found that the pink varieties are the most successful of the singles for holding colour when preserved. The two best are: 'Natalia' – that difficult to find and hard to grow pale pink beauty – and 'Gladys Hepburn', which is the more vigorous of the two and best suited to the cooler areas of the country.

Bougainvilleas which are particularly good for drying are the many new doubles. Anyone who grows them will know their flowers cling to the stem long after they have actually withered, making them ideal candidates for preserving. Popular varieties are the lovely soft pink fused with white, 'Bridal Bouquet', 'Philippine Parade' which changes to a darker pink, and 'Princess Mahara', a dazzling magenta.

Extremely useful material for the vase is provided in autumn and winter by the berrying plants. Two particularly attractive varieties spring to mind and are absolute musts for the arranger – the various members of the cotoneaster family and the *Pyrocanthus angustifolia* 'Orange Charmer', which is covered in bright orange berries for most of the cooler months.

There are a good number of berried plants available (see list below) and among the best

Bougainvillea dried in short pieces make lovely long lasting arrangements.

Bougainvilleas 'Killie Campbell' (left) and magenta and white 'Mary Palmer' (right) form a breath-taking backdrop for a sparkling bed of white petunias.

Two delightful and popular camellias are the soft pink single, 'Jennifer Susan' and the shining white double, 'Polar Bear'.

Camellias provide wonderful cut flowers, as well as attractive dark green and shiny foliage for the vase.

64

is Australia's *Eugenia myrtifolia*, one of the most valuable plants in any garden, having a lovely columnar shape, shiny evergreen leaves, feathery shuttlecock-like flowers and large attractive purple-red berries. The berries keep for several days in the vase.

Indisputably beautiful, the eugenia is also an extremely useful plant, particularly when tall screening is needed. Its variegated form, *Syzigium tritone*, is a fine accent plant – with its striking cream and green leaves tinged with pink.

Although not normally thought of as berried plants, the tropical dracaenas also produce sprays of berries, as do our clivias. The shiny seedheads of these woodland plants, left after the flowers have faded, are most attractive and useful for decoration. Growing easily from seed these 'berries' should be sown after you have no more use for the arrangement – but do remember to remove the outer skin before planting.

No spring garden is complete without some form of blossom to herald the warmer days ahead and these are provided largely by fruit-bearing trees, although there are also many purely ornamental varieties available.

Not suitable for all parts of the country but certainly very successful in the Western Cape, are the apple and pear blossoms. Inland gardeners have to be satisfied with the 'Apple Blossom' Escallonia. This plant is not a fruit tree but provides arching sprays with clusters of the most attractive pale pink blossoms which show up well against its shiny green foliage.

The many prunus varieties are the most valuable source of blossom. They range from such beauties as *P. blireana* 'Moserii' (Moser's plum), which has double pink blossom in spring and spectacular dark bronze-mauve foliage in summer, to *P. persica* (flowering peach) and *P. cerasifera* 'Vesuvius' (the red-leafed cherry plum).

There are many other cherry, peach and plum choices but among the most spectacular is *P. pollardi*. The prettiest blossom produced by any prunus, it has striking velvety pink flowers, up to 3 cm across, and a rich bonus in red summer foliage which starts bursting out amongst the blossom just before it falls.

The Japanese flowering cherry, *P. serrulata*, is another sensational spring performer, with double pink blossoms that bloom earlier than most.

Many of the blossoms are very short-lived but the Japanese flowering quince (*Chaenomeles lagenaria*) is an exception. Its blossoms last for nearly two months from the end of winter. They will even last well in the vase if picked in bud, as these open over a long period.

The leaves of many flowering blossom plants are also important, for their lovely colours include shades from apple green to deep purple, almost brown. They are excellent used in arrangements if the ends are crushed and placed in boiling water for about 10 minutes.

Acid soil-loving plants such as the rhododendrons, azaleas and camellias, together with the magnolias, provide another whole range of colourful blooms which are ideal for use in the vase.

Magnolia blossoms are a sensation in the vase and the Ikebana arrangers in particular have wonderful ways with these dramatic blooms, often using only one to produce a simple but impressive design.

The Star magnolia with its attractive small flowers is particularly suitable for arrangements and it is worth your while, where space permits, to grow both the white and blush pink varieties.

The liliflora and soulangiana varieties are the most successful magnolias for the vase, with flowers lasting up to four days in water. If picked when still in bud the more mature buds will unfold in about two days.

The large creamy-white blooms of the beautiful tree magnolia (*M. grandiflora*) is also successful both in vases and floating bowls. Well-developed buds will open in the vase, while open flowers benefit from being submerged in cold water. Magnolia flowers bruise easily and should be handled with extreme care.

Magnolias enjoy only a slightly acid soil (pH 6,5 – 7,00), so don't overdo it. It is enough to plant them with a fair amount of peat and then mulch every spring.

Camellias need a slightly more acid soil. Ensure that it is well drained and has a high humus content. Whatever you do, be careful not to plant them too deeply; they hate to have their roots totally smothered. Watering is most important for they enjoy being moist – but never too wet.

Although the sasanqua varieties may be grown in the open, other camellia varieties should get some protection, certainly from the midday sun in the dry and hot parts of the country. Humidity is very important to camellias and so the drier the area the more shade they require. Siting is most important for if their situation suits them they will prove to be extremely showy.

Camellias last several days in shallow water or floating bowls and need no treatment. Not only are they extremely attractive but they also have shiny dark green foliage which is useful in arrangements. These shrubs rarely grow more than 4 m tall under garden conditions but when happy produce a mass of flowers.

Whereas most acid-loving plants enjoy some shade, the beautiful leptospermums which are natives of New Zealand and Australia love the sun and, strangely, are also drought resistant.

These excellent shrubs for gardens all over the Republic have their arching stems covered in dainty blossoms for many months of the year and provide ample pickings for the vase.

Another unusual feature of these acid-loving plants, which were discovered by Captain Cook, who is said to have brewed tea from their leaves, is that in their natural coastal habitat – where he found them – they thrive and are well able to take wind and salt sea breezes.

They are happiest when left undisturbed – they hate cultivation, because they have a fine hair-root system close to the soil surface. Loosening soil around tea bushes is the main reason for the cry of so many gardeners that 'Tea bushes always die on me!' They are not the fussy plants many people believe – but like Greta Garbo they want to be left alone.

Plant them with a third peat moss to two thirds soil in a decent sized hole, mulch regularly with peat, pine needles, wattle compost or even tea leaves to keep down weeds and you will have healthy plants which will give you untold joy for many years.

With all plants like the tea bushes which do not like root disturbance, the use of the modern 'plastic mulch' is a good idea. This consists of specially designed black plastic sheets which are available at garden centres. They fit over the top of the soil around the plant, preventing weed growth and you can cover them with normal mulches to keep the soil acid.

Among the many modern teabush hybrids are single and double forms in pink, white and red. Good named varieties are: 'Blossom', double pink with dark centre; 'Crimson Glory', large double crimson flowers; 'Fascination', bi-coloured pale and dark pink; 'Jubilee', very dark double pink; 'Lambethii', showy two-toned free flowering pink single; 'Pink Pearl', with pearly pink buds that open to pure white flowers; 'Red Damask', one of the oldest and still most popular being free-flowering double red with foliage that changes colour in winter and finally 'Sunraysia', a large double pink which later turns to deep rose.

Arranged in a specimen vase, just a few short sprays of tea bush – pink and 'Red Damask' make a delightful but simple arrangement. Tea Bush sprays last about five days.

CRAB-APPLES

For large and small arrangements the most delightful spring blossoms are provided by those hardy flowering crab-apple trees.

Ideal for the cooler parts of the country, but reasonably successful even in places as warm as Pretoria, crab-apples are truly one of the delights of the spring garden.

Overseas there are a great many crab-apple varieties, but in South Africa they number but a few. Fortunately, one of the most beautiful of them all is *Malus floribunda*, the Japanese crab-apple. A mass of white flowers which start life as glorious crimson buds, a full-grown tree in bloom is a breathtaking sight. Of particular interest is the trunk of these trees – silky smooth, with mottled grey bark, especially noticeable on standard forms.

Grown singly or in groups with other trees, crab-apple foliage offers a good contrast to plants with darker green or silver leaves.

All crabs are deciduous and hardy and the most resistant to cold of all flowering trees. Unfussy about their soil, the majority vary in size between 4,5 m and 7,5 m, with a similar spread when mature.

One of the joys of the crabs is that they often flower in their first year. After their long winter sleep, just before their leaves unfurl, flowers are borne in clusters that entirely cover the branches. In summer the trees are almost as attractive as they are in spring, with their fruits – varying in colour depending on the species – clustered along the branches.

Although not always easy to come by, other particularly attractive crabs worth seeking out are: *M. purpurea* 'John Downie', whose pure white semi-double flowers give way to brilliant orange fruits; *M. purpurea* 'Aldenhamensis', wine-coloured flowers, followed by purple-red fruits in autumn; *M. rosaceae* 'Astrosanguinea', a shrub with spreading habit which has crimson buds, turning to reddish-purple flowers. It has purple-tinted foliage and in autumn produces small yellow-red fruits.

Flowering for two to three weeks, *M. floribunda* is an excellent choice for the vase. Needing no special treatment it does best when cut in bud. Just a few snippets of blossom make for a charming arrangement, and need nothing more than a few of their own leaves to complement them.

Crimson buds turn to detergent white flowers, making the Japanese crab apple one of the most glorious of all the members of the large Malus family.

Although the long crab apple stems, covered in bloom, are ideal for large decorations, only a few snippets were chosen for this arrangement. Flowering for three weeks in warm climates and longer in cooler areas, crabs make excellent cut flowers and need no special treatment, except that it is best to cut them for the vase while they are still in bud. An unusual feature of this arrangement is that two tiny vases in combination were used on a silver salver. The largest vase is only 10 cm tall and the glass has a soft pinky tinge and is known as cranberry glass.

Some useful shrubs, trees and climbers which provide flowers or berries for the vase are:

SHRUBS

Abelia var.
Apple blossom (*Escallonia rubra*)
Azalea
Beauty bush (*Kolkwitzia amabilis*)
Bloukappies or purple broom (*Polygala virgata*)
Blushing bride (*Serruria florida*)
Bouvardia
Buddleia var.
Camellia
Ceanothus
Cestrum var.
Chilean heath (*Fabiana imbricata*)
Chinese hat plant (*Holmskoldia*)
Coffee jasmine (*Murraya exotica*)
Confetti bush (*Coleonema pulchrum*)
Cotoneaster var.
Crab-apple (*Malus*)
Crane flower (*Strelitzia reginae*)
Deutzia
Diplacus
Elderberry (*Sambucus* varieties)
Euryops virgineus
False holly (*Osmanthus*)
Flowering cherry (*Prunus* var.)
Flowering peach (*Prunus* var.)
Flowering plum (*Prunus* (var.)
Flowering quince
Forsythia
Gardenia
Geraldton wax (*Chamaelaucium uncinatum*)
Grevillea juniperine 'Rubra'
Heath (*Erica* var.)
Hibiscus var.
Hydrangea
Indian hawthorn (*Raphiolepis indica*)
Japanese flowering quince (*Chaenomeles lagenaria*)
Japanese sacred bamboo (*Nandina domestica*)
Kerria japonica
Lavender (*Lavandula* species)
Leucadendron var.
Leucospermum (*Protea*) var.
Lilac (Syringa)
Lion's ear (*Leonotis leonurus*)
Magnolia var.
May var. (*Spiraea*)
Mock orange blossom (*Philadelphus*)
Pincushion protea var. (*Leucospermum* species)
Plumbago capensis
Poinsettia var. (*Euphorbia pulcherrima*)
Purple Broom or Bloukappies (*Polygala virgata*)
Purple cestrum (*Iochroma tubelosa*)
Pussy willow (*Salix caprea*)
Rhododendron

Rosemary (*Rosmarinus officinalis*)
Shrimp plant (*Beloperone* var.)
Spanish Broom (*Spartium junceum*)
Tamarisk (*Tamarix* species)
Veronica (*Hebe*)
Viburnum var.
Weigela (*Diervilla*)
Wild dagga (*Leonotus leonurus*)
Wild phlox (*Sutera*)
Wild rhubarb (*Acanthus mollis*)

BERRIES

Amatangulu (*Carissa* species)
Ardisia crenulata
Berberis
Beauty berry (*Callicarpa*)
Clivia
Coral berry (*Symphoricarpos orbiculatus*)
Cotoneaster
Dovyalis caffra
Dracaena
Duranta
Elaeagnus
Firethorn (*Pyracantha angustifolia*)
Golden dewdrop (*Duranta plumieri*)
Hawthorn (*Crataegus lavallei*)
Holly (*Ilex* var.)
Mahonia
Mountain Ash (*Sorbus aucuparia*)
Natal Plum (*Carissa* species)
Osmanthus hetrophyllus
Pernettya mucronata
Photinia var.
Pittosporum
Privet (*Ligustrum* species)
Rhamnus spp.
Snowberry
Stranvaesia davidiana
Strawberry tree (*Arbutus unedo*)

BLOSSOM

Apple blossom (*Escallonia*)
Cherry blossom (*Prunus* species)
Crab-apple (*Malus* species)
Flowering quince (*Chaenomeles lagenaria*)
Mock Orange (*Philadelphus*)
Peach blossom (*Prunus* species)
Plum blossom (*Prunus* species)

TREES

Alberta magna
Amatangulu (*Carissa grandiflora*)
Coral Tree (*Erythrina corallodendron*)
Dombeya
Flowering Gum (*Eucalyptus*)
Frangipani (*Plumeria*)
Golden rain tree (*Koelreuteria paniculata*)
Kaffirboom (*Erythrina caffra*)
Natal plum (*Carissa grandiflora*)
Tree magnolia (*M. grandiflora*)

Tulip tree (*Liriodendron*)

CLIMBERS

Bougainvillea
Clerodendron (*Clerodendrum splendens*)
Clematis var.
Coral creeper (*Antigonon leptopus*)
Delicious monster (*Monstera deliciosa*)
Honeysuckle (*Lonicera* species)
Jasmine var.
Mandevilla suaveolens
Rose var.
Stephanotis floribunda
Wood rose (*Ipomoea tuberosa*)

IX *Fabulous foliage*

The success of foliage arrangements lies in the variety of contrasting colour and texture you find in the garden. Anyone planning a garden for the vase should bear this in mind and try to acquire as many different varieties of shrubs as possible to provide winter colour. For this arrangement, cuttings from a number of shrubs no garden should be without were used: (1) *Prunus nigra* for its dark wine-coloured foliage;   (2) *Elaeagnus pungens* for yellow and lightness;   two abelias – (3) the glossy variety and (4) 'Francis Mason', with striking yellow-green colouring;   (5) the Heavenly bamboo (*Nandina domestica*), lovely feathery foliage which changes colour with the season and   (6) the aspidistra. Considered an old-fashioned plant, the latter is nonetheless valuable in flower arranging. When rubbed with a little vegetable oil the leaves take on a glow. In the garden they make delightful dark green clumps under trees while also being extremely successful plants for dark places in the home. Of particular importance to the arrangement is the trailing yellow-green foliage of the fast growing (7) variegated honeysuckle with its curving lines and (8) the pink *Berberis* 'Rose Glow' which is an excellent shrub to grow, even in the smallest townhouse garden.

Although made up mainly of foliage, one flower was used – a green hydrangea (9). One of the charms of hydrangea flowers is that in autumn, after a glorious summer of colour, they fade to russet hues if left on the bush. Being heavy, the flower was used low down in the arrangement as a focal point. For lightness a second point of interest was provided by (10) agapanthus seedheads. The pods of these were removed for an airy, spiky effect near the top of the arrangement.

Except for removing the seedheads from the agapanthus, the only other material which needed preparation for the vase was the prunus and the hydrangea. With prunus it is important to crush ends of stems or to shave them slightly before dipping their ends into boiling water for five minutes. Slitting the ends of the hydrangea stems and dipping them into boiling water for a short time also keeps them fresh longer.

Charm and character are given to a garden by its background of foliage plants – it cannot merely present a pretty face of flowers.

The brightness and touch of gaiety offered to the border by both annual and perennial flowers, while important, is of a transitory nature and even they are set off to greater advantage by that all important background of permanent plants.

The well planted garden and the one that is most useful to the flower arranger is the one that stands the rigours of winter – the garden that can look good and provide material for the vase when all else is bleak and dreary.

Foliage comes in all colours from white to the darkest green – almost black – of a forest fir. In between are a thousand hues including greys and purples, reds and browns, coppers and silvers, yellows, oranges.

The dense dark-purple foliage of the beautiful *Berberis atropurpurea* 'Nana' provides generous cuttings for the flower arranger.

eraria with its silver-white felt-like filigree leaves which can be used to light up a bronze or purple *Berberis atropurpurea* 'Nana' with its multitude of small rounded leaves. There are really so many lovely shapes and textures: from the deeply indented leaves of the wild rhubarb (*Acanthus mollis*) and the shiny round leaves of Burford's holly (*Ilex cornuta* 'Burfordii') to the great Zulu shield-like leaves of the wild banana (*Strelitzia nicolai*) and the dainty laciness of meadow rue (*Thalictrum aquilegifolium*).

Arrangers soon learn that there is little in the garden that is not usable. What is more, when there is not a single flower in the garden it is still possible to decorate the house in great style with foliage.

The success of a foliage arrangement depends on the variety of contrasting colours and textures one is able to find in the garden, so anyone planning their plot should try to acquire as varied a collection as possible.

For the mini-garden there are a number of small-leafed shrubs which do not spread too much and which provide charming contrasting colours. A good choice for contrasts with pinks and purples would be some of the berberis varieties. The small cotoneasters with their dark shiny leaves and the many euonymus varieties, (two delightful small ones being 'Emerald Gold', with yellow variegations, and 'Emerald Silver') combined with white. Another useful dwarf

Variegated privet (*Ligustrum lucidum* 'Marginatum Aurea' Tricolor).

There are in addition many variegated plants such as the ivies (*Hedera canariensis* 'Variegata', the lovely bright crotons of Natal, periwinkle (*Vinca major* and *V. minor*) and particularly geraniums. There are also many common plants with variegated forms, such as the privet (*Ligustrum lucidum* 'Marginatum Aurea' Tricolor), oleander (*Nerium oleander*) and the Chinese lantern (*Abutilon megapotamicum* 'Variegata').

Remember, it is not only that the foliage colour is important but the subtle blending of textures and forms as much as colour. Even colour can bore!

When designing your garden consider more than just the flowers of a shrub or plant. Study its form and leaves – whether fine or feathery, delicate or bold – and remember that while it is a good idea to have groups of annuals or perennials together, you need to take care over the selection of the bigger plants. A large group of monot-onous dark green shrubs, such as *Viburnum sinensis*, may look very dull alone, yet one fine specimen grouped with plants of varying colours and shapes may look stunning.

Nor is it only the large plants that have interesting textures; you can create striking effects with such light and airy foliage as that provided by the herb dill, in company with the more substantially leafed golden euonymus (*E. japonicus* 'Aureus').

Indeed, one of the delights of landscaping is the combining of plants to create effects which please you – and the choice of material is enormous. Try a furry-leafed *Phlomis fruticosa*, a shrubby evergreen with grey-green leaves and yellow nettle-like flowers, with a rather spiky 'Rosemary McConnel's Blue'. Useful contrast material is the *Senecio cin-*

Purples and browns are useful foliage colours for contrasting with greens and yellows in the garden and they also provide masses of cutting material. This prunus is an excellent example.

72

variety is the little *Eugenia myrtifolia* 'Globulus' which has shiny dark green leaves tinged with red.

For the picture on page 70, a good mixture of material was gathered from one small townhouse garden. Included are: *Prunus nigra* for its dark wine colour; *Elaeagnus pungens* for yellow and lightness; two different abelias, the ordinary glossy variety (*A. cupestris*) and *A.* 'Francis Mason' for their golden-green hues. The creeper in the arrangement is the variegated honeysuckle (*Lonicera japonica* 'Aurea Reticulata'), which is useful as much for its beautifully curving lines as for its interestingly veined green and gold leaves. Adding a touch of pink to the whole is *Berberis* 'Rose Glow'.

Two other plants used in the arrangement are a must – for anyone interested in foliage – the aspidistra and Japanese bamboo (*Nandina domestica*), the first for its shiny, broad dark strap-like leaves and the other for its lovely feathery foliage.

The nandina adds not only lightness to an arrangement, but also colour. Its leaves offer a tremendous range of autumn tints.

Though considered an old-fashioned plant, the aspidistra is worthy of a place in even the smallest garden. While it is delightful in dark green clumps under trees, it is also useful in the house as a pot plant – growing even in dim conditions. A little vegetable oil applied to aspidistra leaves gives them an attractive glow. Their bold leaves are also useful for dry arrangements.

Although consisting mainly of foliage, the accompanying arrangement also includes one flower and some spent flower heads. The flower is the 'green' hydrangea. One of this plant's charms is that in autumn, after a glorious summer of colour, its flowers fade to lovely greens and russet hues if left on the bush.

Among the spent flower heads in the arrangement are the lovely little russet to lime green calixes of the glossy abelia, left behind when the flowers die. They add interest to an arrangement when no blooms are available. Attractive at all times of the year, abelias supply delicate small flowers for a long spell during the warm months.

The second set of 'heads' is that of the agapanthus. They have had their seed pods removed to make them look like fascinating spiky green flowers and this produces an airy effect near the top of the arrangement.

Besides removing the seeds from the agapanthus, the only other material which needed some preparation for the vase was the prunus and the hydrangea.

It is important to crush ends of prunus stems or to shave them slightly before standing them in about 3 cm of boiling

Abelia 'Francis Mason', the brightest member of a very useful shrub family, with striking yellow-green foliage and dainty pink flowers, produces arching branches ideal for large arrangements as well as many small snippets suitable for mini vases.

Berberis 'Rose Glow', with its pink and purple foliage, contrasts well with the gold-green of the Golden elderberry (*Sambucus nigra* 'Aurea'). Both shrubs are musts for the arranger's garden.

73

water for five minutes. Slitting the ends of hydrangea stems and dipping them in boiling water for a short time keeps them fresh for a long time; adding powdered alum to the water also helps.

Although the 'cuttings' used in this arrangement were not supported, a pincushion holder was placed in the bottom of the vase to support the stems which constitute the frame.

Foliage for your arrangements may be gathered from all corners of the garden and even grasses from an overgrown pavement – if you admit to one – may be used. Sources include the herb garden, shrubs, trees, climbers, perennials and even groundcovers, one of the most used foliage items being the common periwinkle, both green and variegated.

Trailing plants are of course very important in the arranger's garden and an extremely useful one, whether grown as creeper or groundcover, is the common green ivy. This wonderful evergreen presents itself in a variety of forms ranging from those with wavy leaves, such as 'Curlilocks', to the many coloured forms, including 'Glacier' with its shadings of silver and white and 'Golden Heart' which has a bright yellow centre.

South African arrangers are fortunate that one of the most useful filler materials for floral designs is our indigenous family of asparagus ferns, which in most places grow like weeds. Their variety of colour and form is remarkable, varying from the dark green feathery *A. plumosus* to the yellow-green of the rather stiff cat's tail asparagus (*A. meyerii*) and, most useful of all, the *A. sprengeri*, which is marvellous for baskets or for tumbling over banks or for softening the edges of terraces.

Nor is the charm of sprengeri in its foliage alone. In autumn it produces masses of minute white fragrant flowers which later turn to bright red mini-tomato-like berries. This tough filler lasts very well – even without water, so that it may be used as is in table decorations and many other places and will look fresh and lovely for several days.

Another useful form is the light green smilax. The advantage of these plants is that they grow equally vigorously in open ground or container. This makes them ideal for people with small properties and may even be grown successfully by flat dwellers on balconies, either in containers or hanging baskets.

One of the densest picking areas is of course from the plants around the borders of your garden and when choosing your

Cat's tail asparagus can provide the odd plume for an arrangement but regard it as a light picking area to be used only for special occasions or you will ruin the shape of the bush.

FERNS

Few people ever think of ferns as anything but house plants, yet these feathery beauties thrive in the great outdoors and not only give a lush, tropical appearance to shady areas of the garden, but also provide a wonderful crop of picking material.

Delicate they may look, but in fact ferns are fairly tough and given their few simple requirements do extremely well.

In the garden their needs are:

- partial shade.
- moist but not wet conditions.
- good drainage. A gently sloping position is ideal.
- loose and friable soil which contains quantities of peat moss, leaf mould and compost.
- the crown of the plant should never be covered with soil.

Given these requirements ferns flourish, creating a delightful woodland scene in a shaded garden setting.

Although ferns no longer dominate the view from the bay window or cascade from tall planters as they did in Victorian times, they are today possibly more popular than they have ever been.

The range of fern varieties is vast and includes those charming little button ferns (*Pellaea rotundifolia*), the epyphytic staghorns with their antler-like fronds, and the majestic tree ferns (*Cyathea*). A visit to your local nursery or garden centre can be an eye-opening experience.

With more than 10 000 fern species to choose from, it is not surprising that this is one of the most exciting plant families in the world. However, less than a 100 varieties are grown widely, let alone 10 000. Nevertheless, there are a number of ferns which are easy to propagate, which will be of use to the flower arranger and which grow successfully out of doors in most South African garden situations.

These include those dainty maidenhair ferns (*Adiantum*) with their fine feathery foliage; miniature tree ferns (*Cyathea blechnum gibbun*); holly fern (*Cyrtomium falcatum*); Bird's nest fern (*Asplenium nidus*); the common sword fern (*Nephrolepsis exaltata*) and the Boston fern (*N. bostoniensis*).

Also very attractive in the garden are the many varieties of *Pteris* ferns, with *P. pactra*, the leather leaf or florist's fern being particularly popular with arrangers because of its long life in water. South African growers who export this fern overseas claim that it lasts anything up to six weeks after cutting.

Worth considering among the more unusual yet easy to grow ferns is the Rabbits' foot fern (*Davallia fijiensis*), which has dense, dark green carrot-top-like foliage and furry surface roots from which it gets its name. This species is excellent for growing in baskets.

Ferns may be used for many purposes in the garden but look particularly attractive when grown around pools and waterfalls, in damp grottoes and on banks of ponds and streams. They are ideal in shady rock gardens and also excellent groundcovers under trees.

For the gardener who desires a tropical look in the garden, nothing creates the lush natural forest-like appearance better than

Gardening with ferns, whether it be for lush effect on a patio or under trees in the garden, is a rewarding pastime for the arranger.

the underrated fern, while for the arranger they supply a never-ending source of filler material.

Grouping a variety of potted ferns in a shady corner or on the patio can be very effective, giving a lovely cool, leafy effect.

Though not a fern, the unfortunately named tape-worm plant (*Muehlenbeckia platyclados*) is a most attractive and charming addition to any fernery. It can grow fairly large and is capable of producing masses of cuttings for the vase.

screeners always consider their value for this purpose. There are many extremely useful varieties but among the very best as regards density, beauty of leaf and 'cutability' are the various viburnums (*V. sinensis*, *V. tinus* 'Lucidum', *V. tinus* 'Lauristinus' and even the variegated form, *V. tinus* 'Variegata'.

Other very attractive and useful screening shrubs are the variegated privet (*Ligustrum lucidum* 'Marginatum Aurea' (tricolor), the brush cherry (*Eugenia myrtifolia*) and its variegated form *(Syzigium tritone)*, *Photinia davidsoniae* and its more colourful forms, *P.* 'Red Robin' and *P. glabra* 'Rubens' with lovely reddish young growth.

Gardeners new to flower arranging tend to think of foliage colour in the garden as being mainly green, bronze or yellow, but in fact there is a whole range of other useful colours worth including in your scheme. One that should not be overlooked is the green and white range offered by such shrubs as *Myrtus communis* 'Variegata', *Coprosma bauerii marginata* and in particular the variegated lemon wood (*Pittosporum eugenoides variegatum*), which has dense pale green leaves with silver margins.

All the pittosporums provide wonderful picking material, but one particularly charming member of the family is *P. nigricans*

with its lovely pale green leaves which show up against very dark stems. Its scented maroon flowers are a bonus.

The New Zealand flax plant (*Phormium tenax*) is another extremely useful choice for an accent position, being very striking with a white stripe to its long, grass-like leaves.

Most of the silver-leafed plants are rather small and include senecio, *Artemesia* 'Lam-

This small bed provides a fair range of foliage plants from Egyptian papyrus (left) to palm fronds and elephant ears – all useful for dramatic, large arrangements.

brook Silver', *Cineraria maritima*, Lamb's ears (*Stachys lanata*) and *Santolina chamaecyparissus*. Wonderful exceptions to this are the penny or florist's gum and the sparkling silver tree of the Cape (*Leucadendron argenteum*). Although fronds of this beauty are extremely useful, one must be careful not to spoil it by over-picking.

Another wonderful foliage colour to include in your arrangements is pink, but it is not easy to find. Exceptions, however, are the Pink May (*Spiraea bumalda* 'Anthony Waterer') with its lovely pink-tinged green-yellow leaves and pink flowers, and the previously mentioned 'Rose Glow' berberis.

Another blush-tinged beauty is the Ice cream bush, *Breynia disticha* 'Roseo-picta' (*syn. Phyllanthus nivosus* 'Roseo-picta') with its beautifully-coloured leaves – white, pale green and shades of pink. This plant is very short-lived; submerging its stem-ends in boiling water for a few minutes will prolong its life a little, but it rarely lasts more than a day or so.

Some of the most colourful foliage of all appears in autumn when leaves start to turn. This will be discussed in the chapter on the 'Seasons'.

Practically any area of the garden will provide foliage material for the vase, but one of the richest sources is, oddly, the herb garden, being a particularly useful source of light and interesting leaf shapes. These include the lovely yarrow (*Achillea millefolium*) with its profusion of fern-like grey leaves and white and pink clusters of flowers. Useful too is fennel, which has feathery thread-like leaves and attractive umbels of flowers. Not to be overlooked are the many forms of lavender, the various scented geraniums, borage and dill.

For foliage you can collect virtually anything from old palm leaves to those gorgeous young leaves of the delicious monster (keep this a light picking area unless you have a real monster of a monster). Even the water garden will provide you with foliage: *Pontederia cordata*'s assegai-like leaves last in the vase for at least a week. Very useful too are the various water grasses and Egyptian papyrus.

Exciting colouring makes the Ice-cream bush *Breynia disticha* 'Roseo-picta' *(syn. Phyllanthus nivosus* 'Roseo-picta') a very desirable shrub for the warmer gardens where it will grow, but unfortunately it is not a great success in the vase. Putting stem ends in boiling water helps but it rarely lasts longer than a day.

The silver-foliaged Lamb's ear (*Stachys lanata*) not only produces a dense groundcover but is an excellent contrast plant for the vase.

Useful foliage plants for the flower arranger planning a garden:

PINK TINTED

Berberis 'Rose Glow'
Caladium
Flowering quince (*Chaenomeles*)
Geralton wax (*Chamaelacium uncinatum*)
Hypericum moserium
Icecream bush (*Breynia disticha* 'Roseo-picta'
    (syn. *Phyllanthus nivosus* 'Roseo-picta'))
Japanese bamboo (*Nandina domestica*)
Prunus glandulosa
Prunus species
Raphiolepis indica
Serruria florida
Syzigium tritone

YELLOW

Abelia 'Francis Mason'
Bambusa 'Golden Goddess'
Coprosma 'Coffee Cream'
Coprosma picturata
Chinese lantern (*Abutilon megapotamicum*
    'Variegata')
Elaeagnus pungens
Euonymus varieties
Geelbos (*Leucadendron adscendens*)
Geranium varieties
Golden elder (*Sambucus racemosa* 'Plumosa
    aurea')
Golden privet (*Ligustrum ovalifolium*
    'Aureum')
Gold striped century plant (*Agave angusti-
    folia* 'Marginata')
Hen-and-chickens (*Chlorophytum comosum*
    'Variegatum')
Holly (*Ilex aquifolium* 'Golden Queen')
Honeysuckle (*Lonicera japonica* 'Aureo-
    Reticulata')
Ivy varieties (*Hedera* species)
Japanese laurel (*Aucuba japonica*)
Sansevieria var.
Spider plant (*Chlorophytum comosum*
    'Variegatum')
Zebra grass (*Miscanthus sinensis*)
Variegated holly (*Ilex aquifolium* 'Vari-
    egatum')
Veronica (Hebe var.)

CREAM

Chinese lantern (*Abutilon savitzii*)
Coprosma 'Coffee Cream'
Coprosma 'Marble chips'
Flax (*Phormium* varieties)
Hen-and-chickens (*Chlorophytum comosum*
    'Variegatum')
Liriope muscari 'Variegata'
Pittosporum eugenioides 'Variegatum'

Variegated privet (*Ligustrum lucidum* 'Mar-
    ginatum Aurea')
Veronica varieties (*Hebe* species)

SILVER AND GREY (BLUE)

Artemesia
Caryopteris
Centaurea
Cotoneaster varieties
Dianthus 'Doris'
Everlasting (*Helichrysum angustifolium*)
Florist's gum (*Eucalyptus cinerea*)
Globe artichokes
Honesty (*Lunaria*) silver seed pods
Lavender (*Lavandula* species)
Nepeta
Penny gum (*Eucalyptus cinerea*)
Perovskia atriplicifolia
Rosmarinus officinalis
Ruttya graveolens
Santolina chamaecyparis
Senecio cineraria
Stachys lanata

PURPLE

Acer palmatum 'Atropurpureum'
Berberis varieties
Canna
Castor oil plant (*Ricinus communis*)
Copper beech (*Fagus sylvatica* 'Cuprea')
Copperleaf (*Acalypha wilkesiana*)
Icecream bush (*Breynia disticha* 'Roseo-picta'
    (syn. *Phyllanthus nivosus* 'Roseo-picta'))
Lobelia cardinalis
Mahonia
Prunus varieties
Purple dragon palm (*Cordyline australis*
    'Atropurpurea')
Purple flax (*Phormium tenax* 'Atropurpurea')
Smoke bush (*Cotinus coggygria*)
Wandering Jew (*Zebrina pendula*)

GREEN

Virtually ninety per cent of all plants produce green foliage, but there are those which for a variety of reasons, are particularly useful for arrangements. Some plants last well in the vase, some are floriferous or have interesting and varied shapes. Here are some of the most useful plants:

Abelia varieties
Asparagus varieties
Aspidistra lyrida
Bergenia cordifolia
Bamboo varieties
Brush cherry (*Eugenia myrtifolia*)
Choisya ternata
Cordyline varieties
Cotoneaster varieties

Delicious Monster (*Monstera deliciosa*)
English laurel (*Prunus laurocerasus*)
Fern varieties
Flax (*Phormium* varieties)
Iris
Ivy (*Hedera* species)
Hosta varieties
Mirror bush (*Coprosma baueri*)
Myoporum laetum
Myrtle (*Myrtus communis*)
Nasturtium (*Tropaeolum*)
Papyrus antiquorum
Periwinkle (*Vinca major* and *V. minor*)
Photinia varieties
Pittosporum varieties
Osmanthus ilicifolius
Sacred bamboo (*Nandina domestica*)
Shepherd's holly (*Osmanthus ilicifolius*)
Spider plant (*Chlorophytum* varieties)
Tape-worm bush (*Muehlenbeckia platyclados*)
Thalictrum varieties
Viburnum varieties
Wild banana (*Strelitzia nicolai*)
Wild rhubarb (*Acanthus mollis*)
Wild strawberry (*Duchesnea indica*)

Not only the colour, but also the nature of the foliage is of importance to the flower arranger:

BOLD LEAVES

Aralia sieboldii
Artichoke (*Cynara cardunculus*)
Arum lily varieties (*Zantedeschia* species)
Aspidistra
Bergenia
Canna
Castor oil plant (*Ricinus*)
Crotons (*Codiaeum* varieties)
Cycad varieties
Cycas revoluta
Delicious Monster (*Monstera deliciosa*)
Fatsia japonica
Hosta
Lotus (*Nelumbo nucifera*)
Mother-in-law's-tongue (*Sansevieria*
    varieties)

PALM VARIETIES

Philodendron varieties
Rubber plant (*Ficus elastica*)
Strelitzia nicolai and *regina*
Wild rhubarb (*Acanthus mollis*)

FEATHERY LEAVES

Astilbes
Asparagus varieties
Bamboo varieties
Bracken (*Pteris aquilena*)
Celosia plumosa

Chamomile (*Matricaria chamomilla*)
Erica varieties
Fern varieties
Lavender varieties (*Lavandula* species)
Santolina
Water grass (*Cyperus alternifolia*)
Tamarix

LACY LEAVES

Artemesia pontica
Dill
Fennel
Maidenhair fern
Thalictrum varieties
Lace flower (*Didiscus caerulius*)
Lovage (*Levisticum officinale*)
Rabbit's Foot fern
Sacred bamboo (*Nandina domestica*)

TRAILING FOLIAGE

Asparagus varieties
Clematis varieties
Hen and chickens (*Chlorophytum comosum*)
Honeysuckle varieties (*Lonicera* species)
Ivy geranium
Ivy varieties (*Hedera* species)
Periwinkle (*Vinca major* and *V. minor*)
Rhoicissus tridentata
Star jasmine (*Trachelospermum jasminoides*)
Stephanotis floribunda
Virgina creeper

Not all these plants will grow in all parts of
South Africa and the best way of finding out
exactly which will suit your particular area
is to visit your local nurseryman with a list
of those that interest you. He will very soon
put you right.

White and green, yellow and purple, pink and almost
black green – the range of foliage colours is infinite.

X Matchless musts

Wouldn't everyone love to garden with all the plant varieties suitable for the vase – what a garden one would have! While there are simply far too many to include them all, there are some plants which no garden should be without. These include, of course, roses, violets, sweet peas, geraniums and berry plants – all of which I have already discussed. In this chapter I shall suggest other varieties which demand inclusion in the arranger's garden, together with a few rather special plants which, although not necessities, will give you a great deal of pleasure.

To begin I will discuss those which few flower arrangers would consider being without – abelia, our indigenous arum lily, azalea, daisy varieties, day lily, frangipani, gypsophila, hibiscus, hydrangea, iris varieties, Japanese anemone and nandina. This will be followed by advice on two of our indigenous plants, proteas and strelitzias, and on that lovely exotic bloom, the peony. These are very rewarding plants and arrangers should try to fit them in if at all possible.

To conclude I shall discuss three annuals which flower arrangers should certainly try to make space for – Honesty (*Lunaria*), which produces wonderful seed pods that dry to form striking silver discs; *Lavatera trimestris*, one of the finest introductions in recent years, and the lovely *Lisianthus russellianus*, a hybrid which was unknown in South Africa before 1984 and which already looks set to take the cut flower trade by storm.

ARUM LILIES

Wonderful companion plants, ideal for popping into any empty spaces in the garden or near a tap, it is surprising that this easy to grow indigenous charmer is not used more often in South African gardens. Arums look equally beautiful grown among impatiens or foliage plants, with agapanthus or ferns. They make excellent cut flowers.

Although in their native Cape arums grow in full sun, they generally prefer a little shade, particularly in hot dry inland areas – doing better under trees or in east-facing positions where they get no afternoon sun. Even on the hot Highveld they will grow in full sun, but generally their flowers do not last well and go brown if the plant is allowed to be dry for even a short time.

At their best arums grow to almost a metre in height, and their dark green arrow-shaped leaves form dense, attractive and neat bushes. The unusual flowers are funnel-like white spathes, which narrow to a point

With only their own leaves as a foil, arums make a striking arrangement. These plants are well worth growing for garden and vase.

Several varieties of protea, including the popular pincushion (*Leucospermum cordifolium*), oleander-leaved protea (*P. nerifolia*) and leucadendrons which give a fascinating foliage effect; some Peach proteas (*P. grandiceps*) and the pink and cream varieties of the common Suikerbos were used here.

This arrangement stands in a copper coal bucket with a setting of attractive copper items. No special treatment was necessary and nothing was used to hold the flowers, but the foliage below the waterline was removed. To show the flowers to greater advantage a few of the leaves surrounding the blooms were also removed. Do not strip off too many leaves, however, as they are attractive and add fullness when you have few stems available.

Arums have it all, they're tall, they're beautiful and they flower and flower. On the bush they last for a long time and keep in the vase for four or five days.

around a prominent yellow spadix. Flowers last on the bush for a long time and even when cut will live for about five days.

Because arums multiply so quickly it is wise to divide them after their second year, during their semi-dormant period in late autumn. Although they grow well even with scant love and attention there is no doubt that they do far better if kept well watered and if given a boost of general fertilizer SR 3:2:1 (28) at the end of winter.

The plants bloom profusely during spring, and then flower intermittently for most of the rest of the year, with a flush of flowers in early autumn.

Their lush, rather glamorous leaves give a tropical look useful not only for the herbaceous border but also for patio plantings and in poolside beds.

Arums grow in a variety of forms and colours. Among the whites is one with a soft perfume and plain green leaves; another has leaves that are speckled white; while there are also some whose flowers open wider than others. In addition there is a variety called the green arum, whose white spathes are tipped with green.

The coloured varieties are sun lovers and include two yellows – a pale and a darker form – and small pinks which grow to a height of 30 cm to 40 cm. They flower in mid-summer and like a well-drained soil, but enjoy a lot of water during their flowering period, prior to going into their long spell of dormancy.

Although arums look well when mixed with other flowers in large arrangements, they are most attractive when arranged on their own with only their leaves for company. Ideal for home decoration they are most useful for large arrangements in

halls and churches, for banquets and weddings.

In the accompanying arrangement a shallow bowl was used as the container. Little treatment was needed for the flowers: they were picked the day before and kept overnight in deep water.

There is a trick to arranging arums, however. Their stems are very straight and to give the decoration a softer and more flowing look, one should curve their stems in advance. There are two ways of doing this. One is to lay the stems in a bowl with a weight across them, the heads protruding over the edge. The second, popular in the Cape, is to remove a 5 cm-long thin strip from the outer skin at the base of the flower stem. Place the stem in deep water overnight and by morning you'll find it has formed an attractive and graceful curve.

Although most people cut arum stems when picking, the correct method is to remove the entire stem from the plant by gently twisting and plucking with a sharp jerk. For this there are two reasons, first, the stem does not bleed away a lot of its juices and thus lasts much longer and, secondly, it prevents the remaining section of the stem from rotting in the plant and causing disease.

A large pin-holder was used in the bowl for this arrangement, with the tallest flowers being used at the back, working forward with flowers of graduated lengths to short stems at the front. It is also best to start with the least open flowers at the back and the widest open at the bottom. A few arum leaves have been used among the flowers and in the front.

HIBISCUS

Instant flower arrangements are the dream of every hostess and one of the most valuable shrubs to include in any garden for this purpose is the hibiscus – preferably a number of them in different colours to suit your interior decorating schemes.

Hibiscus grows in a wide range of brilliant hues, from red and yellow to white and orange, as well as a whole variety of pinks, from the softness of 'American Beauty' with its satiny-textured petals, to 'Agnes Gault', with its deep pink veins and purple throat, and the bold salmon of 'Ross Estey'.

In addition to the many colours there are single and double varieties, huge hybrids and some varieties with smaller flowers which give an excellent show when grown in tubs on decks or patios.

For the accompanying arrangement a light pink variety, 'Canary Island', was used. This is one of the most useful of all the hibiscus, for not only is it floriferous – it never seems to stop flowering from early spring until late summer – but it is a colour which fits in with most home decors.

'Canary Island' is also a good choice for people living in townhouses and penthouses. It is an excellent tub subject and may be trained into a ball of colour at the top of a stem.

Many experts say hibiscus should be cut back severely each winter and this method certainly does produce bigger and better flowers and a very healthy bush, but the flower arranger should remember that this practice delays flowering. Most arrangers prefer to give their bushes a light pruning in order to produce earlier flowers – perhaps slightly smaller blooms but many, many more than by the other method. Although delicate, hibiscus may be grown in cold areas in a warm protected corner.

When planting hibiscus ensure that you dig a big hole, which is well-drained. Fill it with one third compost to two thirds soil, to which has been added a cup of SR 3:2:1 (28) fertilizer (for growth) and a cupful of superphosphate (to encourage flowers). It is also a good idea to include a handful of bone phosphate, for this slow-acting fertilizer will keep the bush happy when the strength of the general fertilizer has declined.

For the flower arranger the joy of hibiscus is that its glorious blooms do not need to be kept in water. Buds start unfurling on the bush at about 7h00 each day and are open by about 10h00. They last 24 hours whether kept in water or dry and need no treatment of any kind.

They are ideal for banquet table decoration, for they may be put on the table at any time of the day and will not wilt before the guests arrive and will still be upright and perky – even if the guests stay on for breakfast! As a bonus, the whole arrangement, from picking to completion, need take no longer than 10 minutes. What more could anyone want?

The secret of hibiscus is to pick the flower that opens on the day you require it, so it is best to gather them just before 10h00 in the morning, when you can see which new unfurling buds are opening and which are going off.

Hibiscus makes a wonderfully romantic arrangement when placed on top of mounded dry gypsophila or rings of *Asparagus sprengerii* – a wonderful garden filler which keeps without water for several days. Such an arrangement may be placed practically anywhere from the centre of dining room table to a coffee table in a lounge. As you will need only five minutes to pick three to five hibiscus and twist three lengths of asparagus into circles, it is possible to make an arrangement moments before your guests arrive.

For a dinner table you can make one central arrangement or two smaller ones to encircle the candlestick. Place a few extra flowers on each napkin for a stunningly beautiful table.

For anyone interested in hibiscus some useful varieties are:

Pink

'Agnes Gault', satin pink with dark veins and purple throat; 'American Beauty', pale pink single; 'Canary Island', pale pink with a cerise eye; 'Mrs George Davis', huge full double flower in bright pink with pinky-beige border; 'Ross Estey', one of the most spectacular, opens orange, turns salmon.

Orange

'D J O'Brien', double scarlet-orange, tall vigorous grower, very reliable; 'Mrs Fairbrass', abundant large double orange flowers; 'Ranakanai', large Hawaiian hybrid, one of the best.

Yellow

'Crown of Bohemia', superb golden yellow with orange-red throat; 'Full Moon', spectacular double lemon yellow; 'Californian Gold', free-flowering, low-growing single maize yellow with red eye; 'Halea Kala', single and double yellow with red throat; 'Miss Betty', compact, free flowering medium-sized shrub, maize yellow flowers.

Red

Single red (*H. rosa* 'Sinensis'), probably the most common, most popular and most free flowering of hibiscus, with bright letter-box red flowers.

Apricot

'Madeleine Champion', single with red eye.

'Canary Island' blooms are not as large as some of the new hybrid hibiscus varieties but what it lacks in size it certainly makes up for in profusion. Flowering non-stop for most months of the year this lovely plant is vital in the flower arranger's armoury.

For a touch of romance at the dinner table what could be more effective than these lovely pink hibiscus ('Canary Island') floating on a mound of misty gypsophila.

DAISIES

Probably because they are the first flowers most children draw, there are few of us who do not continue to love these cheery little flowers throughout our lives.

In South Africa we accept these sun lovers as part of our lives, so it was interesting to observe the way in which John Brookes, the famous British landscaper, responded to their charm when he visited this country in 1983. Although he loved most things about our country there was probably nothing which impressed and delighted him more during his visit than the bright masses of marguerites he saw everywhere. It was his opinion that much greater use should be made of massed groups of daisies in our landscape designs.

There is hardly a time when the daisy is not in flower: they bloom almost as soon as they get their first leaf and continue increasing in size and producing more and more blooms until they are a large mushroom of bright flowers. Finally after about 18

Fading from red-pink to soft pink and producing both colours on a bush at the same time, a new marguerite, which has come to be known as 'Ruby Red' in South Africa, is almost as popular as the common yellow variety.

Pink daisies mirror the pattern of the tiles to give a fresh cheerful appeal to this bathroom.

months, when they have formed rather large bushes, they split apart from sheer exhaustion and need to be replaced.

It is a good idea to take slips and root them regularly so that you always have a number of little plants for popping into empty spaces. They grow so easily from cuttings that they may almost be treated as annuals. Each spring place several cuttings taken from strong green tips in a mixture of river sand and peat. To encourage growth, dip the cut ends in a rooting hormone powder.

Marguerites grow in practically any soil, as long as it is well-drained. They need little attention, but ensure they are well watered, for daisies are not as drought resistant as many people believe.

Without another plant in your garden you can, by cultivating these marvellously rewarding plants, ensure you have colour throughout the year.

For the vase there is never a time when they are not suitable, being as ideal for a simple decoration on a breakfast tray as they are for a centrepiece at a cosy luncheon or grand candle-lit dinner.

Marguerites (*Chrysanthemum frutescens*) come in single and double forms, in white, pink and yellow. None surpasses the single yellow in popularity, although in recent times the new pink, known as 'Ruby Red', is proving a real winner. With their lovely dark flowers, which fade to a light pink, these bushes are most attractive when in full bloom, being almost as floriferous as their yellow cousins.

Of the large flowered white varieties, the best bloomer is the one with the dark centre (*C. frutescens* 'Indian Maid'), but even it cannot outdo the mini variety with the feathery grey-green leaf, known as 'Dainty', which now also has an equally busy blush pink cousin.

Common daisies enliven the most ordinary gardens and should never be left out of even the grandest for, in addition to brightening the great outdoors, they flower at their best in winter when few other plants are in bloom, making them an absolute must for floral decorating.

When picking daisies for arrangements, cut some long stems and some short. Try to gather them in the late afternoon of the day before you need them and stand them overnight in deep tepid water. If you leave some of them in a basin you will find that their stems will bend, taking on the shape of the container, and thus will not have a stiff appearance when arranged. The busy housewife will find that the pleasure of decorating with daisies is that they arrange themselves.

A good idea with daisy arrangements is to retain some of the leaves at the top of the stem, as well as a few other clusters of leaves and some unopened buds.

Another member of the chrysanthemum family which is rewarding, both in the border and the vase, is the Shasta daisy (*C. maximum*).

Growing practically anywhere in South Africa, Shastas flower for a long time – from spring through to summer – and the flowering period may be prolonged by judicious snipping off of dead heads as flowers fade. Shastas are tough and will survive considerable neglect, but given a little tender, loving care will show their gratitude with more and bigger blooms. Today these plants are available in a variety of forms, single and double, small and tall.

The humble Michaelmas daisy has enjoyed a meteoric rise in the popularity stakes in recent years, for hybridization has produced a great range of colours and of sizes – from 15 cm in height to some about a metre tall. All are easy to grow and comparatively trouble-free, with only some of the very tall ones requiring staking. Colours today include pink and lilac, mauve, purple and red. The dainty white varieties remain a must in the flower arrangers' garden.

Blue is a difficult colour to include in the garden, but the daisy family can provide even this: our indigenous *Felicia amelloides*,

Daisies arranged at the top of a candlestick next to the visitor's book in an entrance hall offer a cheery welcome to guests. A small, light plastic bowl was used for the arrangement, held by a blob of florist's clay and secured with two pieces of soft florist's wire. In the bowl a small ball of chicken wire holds the flowers. You need not worry about the wires and bowl being seen – it takes only a few daisies to hide them. When arranging the flowers try to give height to the centre by using the straighter, stronger-stemmed flowers and allow the others to curl over and soften the sides.

White daisies add sparkle to banks and beds and flower profusely, even as tiny plants.

It takes only a handful of daisies to make a simple arrangement in an egg cup on a tray – but what a delightful way to say 'Good morning' to a patient or overnight guest having breakfast in bed.

Flowering for 12 months of the year it is possible with daisies to have arrangements like this even in the depths of winter.

known overseas as the kingfisher daisy is a tender plant best suited to areas where winters are mild. In the right conditions this marvellous groundcover spreads over a large area in a very short time.

Felicias grow into very bushy plants if the leading and side shoots are nipped out when young and for best flowering it is important to remove dead heads. Although perennial, it may be used with great success as a summer annual in cooler areas.

Another popular daisy in South Africa is our indigenous Barbeton, which known by its proper name, *Gerbera jamesonii*, has become one of the top selling cut flowers in Europe.

The simple little red flower that appears on badges as the emblem of Northern Transvaal sports teams has now been transformed by hybridizers into a many coloured beauty.

There are both single and double varieties available, in colours ranging from cream, yellow and soft pink to salmon, rose, orange and red. When growing, these fascinating plants demand one thing – good drainage. Besides this they need only a light soil with quantities of compost.

For most of the perennial daisies it is best to prepare the soil to a depth of about 30 cm and include one cupful of SR 3:2:1 (28) fertilizer and superphosphate to a square metre. No special feeding is necessary, but do keep well watered.

HYDRANGEAS

Hydrangeas flower at their best at Christmas, so it is not surprising they have come to be known in South Africa as Christmas flowers – or *Kersfeesroos* in Afrikaans.

There is hardly a South African garden without these spectacular shrubs which produce masses of flowers during summer and are ideal for flower arrangements during the festive season.

They are not only suitable for large displays but are also perfect for table decorations. With single flower heads up to 40 cm in diameter it is possible to make a fine arrangement with only one bloom.

The most commonly seen variety of hydrangea in South African gardens is *H. macrophylla*, which grows in a large range of colours including white, pink, blue, red and even purple.

They are easy to grow either in tubs or in the ground, and require a lot of moisture – their very name coming from the word 'hydro', meaning water.

Although hydrangeas will grow quite happily in the sun, they do need shade during their flowering period in hot, dry inland areas or their blooms get burned. In most parts of the country they are most successfully grown on the south side of the house or in dappled shade under trees.

Their soil requirements are simple. They prefer a deep rich loam, enriched with a third compost for the pink varieties and a third peat moss for the blue range.

As they are gross feeders large amounts of organic material should be given in the form of a mulch during spring, once growth has started. Extra liquid feeding will also help to produce large colourful blooms. Special hydrangea concentrates are available at garden centres to keep the soil acid.

Hydrangeas will normally retain their colours in neutral soil, but should you find the colours of your plants changing it is possible to control this. For instance white and blue hydrangeas enjoy an acid soil with a pH of between 4,5 and 6,0 and to keep the blooms these colours, sulphur, iron chelate and peat moss may be added to the soil. For pink hydrangeas which enjoy a soil pH of 6,0 to 7,5 add a little agricultural lime to maintain the colour.

To ensure good flowers each year, it is important to prune your plants and this is best done during winter. Cut back to three pairs of buds on mature plants to produce large blooms on sturdy new stems. This method tends to reduce the number of flowers, however, and many arrangers prefer to undertake light pruning in January or February, at the end of the blooming period, as this results in smaller blooms but in larger numbers the following season. It is still important for the health of the plants, however, to cut back severely every few years and to remove all old wood. With new plants it is very important to prune back extensively to ensure a strong foundation of stems.

In addition to the common *Hydrangea macrophylla*, two which are certainly worth having in any garden are the oak leaf hydrangea (*H. quercifolia*) and the tree hydrangea (*H. paniculata*). Both these shrubs are hardy and can endure frost.

Hydrangea quercifolia grows to a height of two metres and has large attractive oak-like leaves which turn a vivid bronze-red in autumn. This hydrangea, unlike the others, may be grown in the sun – even in the hot highlands of the Republic. It produces quantities of large pure white panicles of pointed flowers which, if left on the bush, turn to a pale pink. They are wonderful for flower arranging and dry very well.

Growing to a height of 9 m, *H. paniculata* could be called a tree rather than a shrub. It produces panicles of creamy white flowers, which eventually turn purplish. *H. paniculata* flowers later than most of the other varieties and is an extremely useful plant for those who have the space.

This grand arrangement of hydrangeas specially prepared for a Golden Wedding celebration mirrors the hydrangea pattern of the curtains. A Grecian urn placed on a pedestal forms a strong focal point in this charming room. The attractive foliage with the hydrangeas is the yellow-green elaeagnus and the dark leaves of *Prunus nigra*.

Ideal for cold gardens, *Hydrangea quercifolia* is a fine addition to the shrubbery, with flowers for a long time in summer and colourful foliage in autumn.

The green seedheads left when petals drop from Japanese anemones add a light and dainty touch to this arrangement.

Short pieces of Japanese anemone make a delightful dumpy arrangement.

JAPANESE ANEMONE

One of the most beautiful and useful perennials for garden and vase is the tall Japanese anemone, which flourishes in light shade positions and brightens borders for many weeks at the end of summer and on into autumn.

Over a metre tall, the Japanese anemone is ideal for placing at the back of a border or for edging banks of shrubs. They produce masses of 7,5 cm wide single flowers, either white or pink or double rose. With button-like centres surrounded by a glowing mass of yellow stamens, their long stems rise from a thick crown of large dark green three-pointed maple-like leaves. The shades of anemones are very similar to those of cosmos.

Anemones do not enjoy being moved and are best left for several years in one position, where they multiply rapidly. When it is necessary to divide them – after their flowering period has ended – try to leave the original crown undisturbed, preferably removing the plantlets surrounding it. The job is best done in the cool of the day.

When planting, set 45 cm apart in well-drained soil which includes a lot of compost. Although Japanese anemones will grow successfully in full sun, their attractive leaves are inclined to get burned and they are happiest with a cool root run. They are best planted either under trees with light shade and sun for part of the day or surrounded by other perennials which shade their roots but allow their heads to grow up into the sun.

As cut flowers they are excellent for both fine tall and small low arrangements.

Japanese anemones thrive when grown with their feet in the shade and their heads in the sun.

88

Because they grow on branching stems the flowers are most successful in vases when only the long side stems at the top are slit. These will last from two to four days depending on the weather. For a very tall arrangement, it is possible to use the entire length, including the long main stem, but then the flowers do not last well.

For the best results flowers should be picked the evening before use and stems put into boiling water for five minutes. Stand in deep tepid water overnight. Once arranged you will find they are very thirsty and your vase should be kept topped up. Their long, strong stems are easy to arrange and look particularly attractive in a tall, clear glass cylinder.

One of the charms of this excellent picking flower is that it looks good even after petals begin to fall, for its green seed heads are attractive and lend a light daintiness to the arrangement. As with all flowers, but particularly anemones, it is important to use very clean vases. These should be washed either in bleach or in water to which a capful of ammonia has been added.

The florist's favourite, gypsophila or as they usually call it, 'gyp', adds lightness to arrangements whether in combination with other flowers, (below) or separately (right).

GYPSOPHILA

Not the easiest plant to grow, but arrangers find it very difficult to live without this dainty filler. 'Gyp', as the florists fondly call it, may be used in practically any decoration, from bridal bouquets to posies and buttonholes, large and small arrangements; just a few sprigs create a soft, misty effect.

Gypsophila keeps so well dry that it is a good idea, after using it in a fresh arrangement, to wash off the stems and allow to dry naturally in a vase. It may also be hung up in a basement or cupboard to dry.

Suitable for a wide variety of purposes, 'gyp' keeps from season to season, being particularly useful during winter when flowers are in short supply. Be careful when handling it, though; its stems are very brittle. When preparing fresh gypsophila for the vase always strip the stems to be submerged completely. It is worthwhile keeping a vase of dry gypsophila of varying lengths close at hand in the room in which you prepare your arrangements.

Don't overdo the 'gyp', however, for as delightful as it is in arrangements, one so often sees arrangers simply using it to fill in gaps of poorly arranged flowers. It should complement – not add to the mess.

Sparkling silver discs of Honesty seed heads add lustre to any arrangement but are particularly striking when used in single variety displays as in this picture.

The three L's – *Lunaria annua* Honesty, *Lavatera trimestris* and *Lisianthus russellianus* may all sound rather odd but they are delightful plants which you won't regret making place for in your garden:

LUNARIA ANNUA

A plant which deserves to be better known in South Africa, particularly among the flower arranging fraternity, is *Lunaria annua* (Honesty), also known as the money plant. This easy-to-grow biennial seeds itself so easily that if not controlled it may become a pest. It is unlikely that this will happen in a garden where people enjoy cutting flowers, for it will never get a chance to throw its seed – the charm of the plant being the silver disc-like seed heads which appear in profusion in late summer–autumn.

The seed pods of the money plant should be allowed to age on the plant until brown and may then be hung up in bunches. If left on the plant for too long the pods may be damaged by late rains or eaten by insects. Before use, the outer skin covering the pods should be rubbed off to reveal the translucent discs.

Sprays of Honesty pods are very fragile and need to be handled with care; it may even be necessary to wire them together. The shiny 'coins' may be used to enliven bouquets and vase displays. They also make beautiful arrangements on their own, and large sprays of them grouped together make sparkling Christmas trees when decorated

Seeing the seedheads of Honesty growing on the plant you would never suspect the beauty lying beneath the green sheaths. Although not spectacular plants, with unimpressive little flowers, they should be grown by every flower arranger for the glittering display they make once the bushes or branches have been hung up, allowed to dry and the sheaths have been rubbed off.

with single colour baubles of red, blue or shocking pink.

Honesty plants are often available in garden centres. Alternately seed should be sown in summer for flowering the following spring. Eventually growing to about 90 cm tall, Honesty produces softly scented flowers – purple, pink or white. These are rather attractive but should not be cut for arranging; leave them to turn to seed as it is the shiny dry pods which are particularly charming.

LAVATERA TRIMESTRIS

Generally known as lavatera, this impressive member of the hollyhock family is fast becoming one of South Africa's favourites. It has leapt to the forefront of the bedding scene in a very short space of time since winning a silver cup – highest award ever given an annual plant.

Close on a metre tall, with a fine bushy habit, lavatera should be planted at least 60 cm to 75 cm apart to avoid crowding. They may be used either as individual plants, towards the back of the border, or can be planted in one opulent bed of shiny pink. They flower for six to eight weeks and are soon covered with 8 cm diameter frilly, glistening flowers. Three to five grouped together in a bed make a stunning display, especially when interplanted with roses, 'Pacific Giant' delphiniums or dahlias.

Suitable for summer and winter planting, they seem to be more successful during the drier months, enjoying similar conditions to petunias. As a result they do best during summer in the Western Cape and during winter in the Transvaal.

Lavateras should be planted in well composted soil which contains a sprinkling of SR 3:2:1 (28) fertilizer.

LISIANTHUS RUSSELLIANUS

Too new to have assumed a common name, this wonderful new hybrid bedding plant is another of the annuals which may be planted for either summer or winter flowering, but which seems to be most successful in the drier months.

This flower has not yet had a chance to be tested in South Africa, having just arrived on the international scene, but it promises to become one of the 'big ones'.

Blooming in pink, white or royal purple, in bud it looks rather like a rose, but when

Lisianthus Russellianus is a mouthful of a name for a wonderful new flower which has won its spurs in the florist trade before being introduced to gardeners. Now available in trays from some garden centres, it is claimed by some arrangers to last up to a month in the vase. The white version is extremely useful for bridal work but there are also soft pink and purple varieties available.

Flowering for nearly two months at a time, *Lavatera Trimestris* 'Silver Cup', the plant which a few years ago gained the highest horticultural award ever granted a seedling, provides a sea of colour for the border. Each plant produces dozens of large glistening pink hollyhock-like blooms.

open is like a cross between a tulip and poppy in shape. Borne on long, strong stems, blooms are about 8 cm in diameter and usually provide two cuttings. Plants should be pinched back to the third or sixth node to induce bushiness and to produce the maximum number of stems for cutting.

Good drainage is important for the Lisianthus and it should have a well composted fertile soil.

These plants are best grown in groups of separate colours, but if a mixed bed is necessary or if simultaneous flowering of all colours is required, then the blue should be sown two weeks later than the others.

DAY LILY

There was a time, not so long ago, when day lilies (*Hemerocallis*) were only yellow and orange. This original species is still in many gardens today, but gardeners aware of the modern hybrids would hardly consider cultivating such old-fashioned friends; the modern varieties are far superior.

Colours available today range from pale pink through to red and on to mahogany and from pale yellow to deep orange. They grow in a range of sizes from 45 cm to 1,2 m tall. There are so many varieties flowering at different times that by planting a selection it is possible to have them flowering for most of the year, certainly throughout the warm months.

In addition to colour range, day lilies now have a number of shapes: moth, spider, butterfly, wheel, star, bell and trumpet. There are even varieties which are wind-resistant for those who live at the coast.

Day lilies are not fussy plants but do best in well-drained and well-composted soil. They are sun lovers but will tolerate light shade. In fact, in extremely hot areas it is wise to provide them with some protection from the hot west sun.

Ideal for massed plantings, the larger growing varieties look best at the back of a bed. Day lilies are easy to propagate by division in spring or autumn. Overcrowded clumps need to be separated every four or five years.

These blooms are marvellous for flower arranging. Although each bloom lasts only one day there are many buds crowning each stem and in the vase these will open in rotation.

Single flowers floated in a bowl make an attractive quick luncheon or dinner-table centrepiece. When whole stems are used in arrangements, buds will remain open for several days. To keep the vase looking good, take care to cut out dead heads as each bloom completes its one day of glory.

NANDINA DOMESTICA

This beautiful Japanese plant, known as the Heavenly or Sacred bamboo, is a delightful shrub of many moods.

Changing throughout the year, it is always interesting and always beautiful, the colour of its leaves varying tremendously with the season. It is certainly a shrub no garden, let alone an arranger's garden, should be without.

Starting in spring with lovely fresh green, pink-tipped leaves, the nandina foliage turns from dark green in summer to yellow, orange and finally red in winter. And this is not all – this striking plant with its many stems, multiplying each year, also has flattish heads of white flowers which later turn to red berries.

Fairly new on the scene in South Africa, is a lower growing but much brighter Nandina clone, which is available in most nurseries but is not sold by a specific name. This variety starts life with vivid red leaves that change to burgundy and then green, before finally turning to lovely autumn shades.

Forming attractive 3 m tall dense shrubs with slender cane-like stems the nandina's usefulness for the flower arranger lies not only in its beautiful colouring but in its delightful lacy leaves which add lightness to an arrangement.

Growing in full sun or even in partial shade, the nandina is drought-resistant and grows in practically any soil, but does best in well-composted loam. And the best news for cold area gardeners is that it can survive frost to 12 degrees C.

Used in flower arrangements it needs no treatment at all but lasts best if given a deep drink of water the night before you use it.

Always full of interest, nandina offers flowers, red berries and foliage which is ever-changing from pink-tipped green leaves in spring to dark green in summer and yellow, gold and red in autumn and winter.

Leucadendrons, those strange proteas with unusual and sparse looking flowers, are excellent used as foliage to fill out arrangements of other varieties of proteas.

Only one protea is needed to provide a striking arrangement as is shown in this charming Ikebana design.

PROTEA

Because of their lasting qualities in the vase and as dried flowers, proteas are a must for flower arrangers and are certainly not as difficult to grow as many gardeners believe, and in fact need little attention. Admittedly their requirements are fairly strict, but once these have been provided they thrive and flourish in a way that will delight you and everyone else who sees your garden.

Cutting flowers will do no harm to your protea bush or pincushion, provided you prune as you cut, always keeping in mind the overall shape of the plant. In fact, if you should leave any flowers on the tree or bush, these should be cut off immediately after blooming. Twist off the heads and cut back a good length of stem to keep the plant compact and healthy.

Many people imagine that because proteas come from the Cape winter rainfall area they will not grow inland. In fact they do very well, provided they are given water during the cold months.

What is important when planting proteas is to give them the correct soil mixture; they enjoy a slightly acid soil, with a pH of about 5.5. This is not difficult to do:

• Dig a hole about 75 cm square and mix into it quantities of peat moss, well-rotted compost or leaf mould, to make up about a third of the quantity to two thirds soil.

• Wattle compost or pine needles may also be added to the mixture to increase acidity.

• Avoid use of fertilizer or manure.

• Good drainage is most important – proteas hate wet feet.

Proteas are best planted in full sun and in a position where they have a certain amount of buffeting from the wind. They enjoy breezes and should never be planted in a hot corner or near a wall.

Since proteas have a surface root system, plant in a position where you will not be cultivating the soil. Keep well mulched to   93 avoid the growth of weeds; any disturbance of roots in mature plants, such as 'skoffeling' or weeding, may prove fatal.

By planting a variety of proteas it is possible to have blooms practically the whole year round. Some varieties, such as the pincushions, produce many hundreds of flowers in a season.

It is also wise to plant some of the protea varieties in relays, for some, such as the pincushions (*Leucospermum* species) and the Silver tree (*Leucadendron argenteum*), have lifespans of only 10 years. To keep up a continuous show it is necessary to grow new plants every few years.

Although proteas are considered tender, a great many varieties will grow in fairly chilly places, often losing only a few flowers or leaves in severe frost and recovering rapidly. There are also some, such as the silver bush (*Leucadendron uliginosum*), peach protea

(*P. grandiceps*) and the true sugarbush (*P. repens*) which are hardy.

Even people with small gardens may grow proteas for some varieties, such as the delicate and lovely Blushing bride (*Serruria florida*), are tiny plants. Many others, such as the various pincushions, are scrubby, except in the Cape where they flourish.

In addition to their value as long-lasting cut flowers, the protea species generally make excellent dried flowers and three of the most valuable for this purpose are *P. nerifolia*, *P. barbigera*, the King protea (*P. cynaroides*) and the ordinary sugarbush (*P. repens*).

One of the loveliest of all proteas and easy to grow on the Highveld, the Peach protea (*P. grandiceps*) is a joy in the vase – lasting about a month. Once again a few leaves were removed around the flowers, the better to show them off. Proteas are thirsty and water should be topped up regularly.

IRIS

Today there are so many beautiful modern hybrid irises available that many gardeners collect them as one would stamps or coins.

As exotically beautiful as orchids, they are far easier to grow, make wonderful bedding plants and provide quantities of excellent cut flowers.

New hybrids are always coming on to the market and for these one should keep a keen eye on annual garden shows, although they can be quite expensive, costing R10 or more for a rhizome. Besides these very special plants, there are many wonderful and relatively inexpensive varieties selling for less than R1, available annually at garden centres and nurseries. Study their catalogues, to discover what is available.

If your local nurseryman is unable to help you, hunt through gardening magazines where you will find regular advertisements placed by iris farmers who will be only too happy to send you their catalogues.

The bearded iris, the original old flag (*I. germanica*), still seen in so many gardens together with its many new hybrids, remains the most popular and widely grown of this large and quite complex species. Bearded irises are breathtakingly beautiful, ranging in colour from the palest blues and yellows, whites and bi-colours to deep purple, brown and gold. Having few rivals in the herbaceous border, they are spectacular when planted in islands of colour.

Although many people believe that irises will survive and even put on a show when grown in poor soil, this does not mean they enjoy such conditions. In fact, given well-drained, slightly alkaline soil in which compost and a dressing of superphosphate or bone phosphate (about a handful per square metre) has been included, they will display their pleasure by flowering in the most remarkable way.

For best results the soil for irises should be prepared months, even a year, in advance, although this is not absolutely essential. Soil should be well dug over to a depth of 15 cm to 20 cm. Now make shallow parallel furrows about 8 cm apart, with a small ridge of soil in between. Your iris rhizomes should then be placed rather like saddles over a horse's back, with the roots draped on either side of the narrow ridge. Cover the roots with soil but try to avoid covering the top of the white part of the rhizome where it joins the leaves, as this portion enjoys both sun and air. Deep planting will not harm the plant but will retard flowering.

Do not divide your clumps of irises too often as it may take a couple of seasons after division before they flower again. Separate only when clumps become overcrowded and flowering deteriorates.

When dividing, first cut off leaves in a fan shape about 10 cm from the stem. Now lift the whole plant out of the bed with a fork. Turn the clump over to expose the tangled mess of roots and wash these off under a tap. Cut out all decaying roots and divide into small sections. Choose your new plants from the outside of the clump and discard the old root section. Each unit should have a fairly sizeable piece of rhizome with a fan of leaves attached.

Irises suffer few problems with pests and diseases, but it is a good idea to remove regularly any dead or dying leaves. Not only are they unsightly but they could harbour rhizome rot, a fungus which is prevalent in hot humid conditions. Rhizome rot can be treated with a weak solution of permanganate of potash. Feed irises with a good sprinkling of superphosphate in July and then water well and regularly until they flower in spring.

Irises are companionable plants and look well planted with such perennials as paeonies, lupins, snapdragons and linaria. They combine particularly well with foxgloves, which flower about the same time. One of the great joys of irises is their beautiful silvery grey-green foliage which should always be included with the flowers in an arrangement. Because of their beautiful leaves iris beds always look neat, even when not in flower, and act as a charming foil for neighbouring plants.

Although rather stiff flowers, irises are excellent in the vase, being well suited to upright designs. It is a good idea to cut some stems rather short so that the flowers may be recessed into the design for strong colour interest. Irises are particularly suitable for Ikebana arrangements.

After picking irises, leave them to have a long drink; once they have taken up the moisture it is possible to arrange them in fairly shallow water.

Try to use those with a second bud on the stem, for when the first fades and is removed the second will expand and mature.

Although the bearded iris retains pride of place in most gardens, do not overlook the many other varieties available, such as the Japanese iris (*I. kaempferi*) and *I. stylosa*. Two particularly good iris varieties for cutting are the Louisiana and the Dutch. The lovely Louisiana which enjoys bog conditions and will even grow directly in water, is tall and slender and has a rather ethereal charm. Dutch irises with their lovely flame blue and yellow blooms are most attractive grown in single colour or companion groups where they can enjoy plenty of sun.

The bulbs of these two varieties are usually available at garden centres in March and April. They may be left in the ground from year to year or lifted and replanted each autumn.

Think seriously about your irises, the choice is vast, but don't be overwhelmed by the variety, you will be delighted with whatever you plant. There are too many famous bearded iris varieties to mention all here, but who could resist such fascinating catalogue names as 'Crushed Velvet' (mulberry with white beard); 'Blue Petticoats' (blue on white); 'Deep Fire' (rich velvet red) or 'Smoke Rings' (smoky orchid-mauve peppered on cream) and 'Summer Dawn' (golden yellow with bright red tangerine beard).

Tall-stemmed Louisiana irises are delightful both in the garden and vase.

95

AZALEAS

Free blooming azaleas have in recent years become one of the popular flowering shrubs in the country – even in areas which are theoretically unsuited to their culture, such as the hot Highveld.

Once considered difficult to grow, gardeners have come to realize that they are in fact very easy if given their few simple requirements. These include:

- ample water
- acid soil (pH 4,5–5,5)
- shade when flowering in areas with low humidity
- good drainage

Normally grown in high rainfall areas, it is necessary in drier regions to provide extra moisture, particularly during hot, dry spells, for they are shallow-rooted plants which can dry out quickly. Extra water is especially important from the time they start developing buds in autumn until the end of their long flowering in spring.

As to soil, it is important to provide azaleas with regular mulches of peat to give them the degree of acidity they enjoy especially in spring and autumn. It is also a good idea to provide regular helpings of food specially prepared for this purpose and usually sold as 'hydrangea' food.

When planting it is wise to dig a hole about 75 cm square and 60 cm deep and in it mix one third peat moss with the soil. For those who can afford it – Irish peat is undoubtedly far superior to our local variety. For mulching you may also use pine needles, wattle compost, oak leaves and even tea leaves.

Normally sun lovers – as anyone who has lived in Natal will know – azaleas need some protection from the hot sun during their flowering period, when grown in areas of low humidity. It is not that they will not bloom in the sun but merely that their flowers will either burn, fade or become blown far more quickly than would otherwise be the case. In Pretoria magentas grown in the sun last for about three to four weeks, as opposed to eight if grown in light shade.

Sun is particularly important during the formation of buds in autumn-winter and one way of achieving the perfect balance of sun and shade at the correct times, is to grow azaleas in pots so that they may be moved.

A similar result may be achieved by growing your azaleas under deciduous trees that lose their leaves during winter when the azaleas need the sun, and then come into leaf again when the azaleas are ready to flower. A particularly suitable tree for this purpose is the white stinkwood (*Celtis africana*)

Azaleas make beautiful single variety arrangements but also combine well with other flowers such as orchids and alyssum in a floating bowl.

which is the first tree to lose its leaves in autumn and the first to regain them in spring.

Unfortunately, growing azaleas under trees gives rise to the problem of root competition and so it is wise always to grow azaleas in pots, even when you plan to plant them in the garden. Another good reason for growing them in containers is that they are an acid-loving plant and it is easier to give them their special soil treatment in such circumstances. When sinking your contained plants into the ground under trees:

• Ensure that you have the right size pot for your plant – azaleas come in various sizes, from miniatures about 30 cm tall to those about 2 m tall with a metre spread. (Check with your nurseryman when buying plants.)

• Ensure good drainage. Make several holes in base of tub, cover holes with broken crocks, cover these with river sand and then add your soil.

• Once a year lift the pot to ensure that the tree's roots have not penetrated the holes under the pot.

• Whether in pots or open ground, provide the plant with one third peat moss to two thirds soil when planting.

• Always maintain a good mulch of peat moss on top of the soil, not only to feed and maintain acidity, but to discourage weeds. Azaleas have a very shallow root system which does not like any interference and 'skoffeling' around them should be avoided.

By growing roses and azaleas it is possible to have flowers in the house all year round, for the azalea flowering period nestles neatly between the pruning of your roses in late July and their blooming again in October.

Because they are available in a wide range of colours, it is possible by growing a variety of different azaleas, to prolong their flowering period. Probably the most prolific and favourite azalea is the common magenta, which grows into a large bush and is covered in flowers for nearly two months. Not quite as densely covered during its main flowering spell, the large white variety 'Alba', has the advantage of flowering on and off during summer. Another star among the more old-fashioned varieties is 'Albert and Elizabeth', a small shrub with lovely frilly white flowers margined with salmon pink. It has a long flowering spell lingering on into summer.

New varieties available today are a breed called the 'Wonder Azaleas', which have been developed in New Zealand. Among them is the lovely soft pink 'Little Girl' which has enjoyed a rapid rise to fame since its introduction to this country in the early 1980s.

White *Azalea* 'Alba' has a long flowering spell with a strong flush at the end of winter and into spring but also continues flowering on and off during summer.

Azaleas make excellent cut flowers, lasting for several days in the vase if conditioned by crushing stems and leaving in deep cold water overnight.

Likely to become even more popular is 'Only One Earth', a rich cherry red azalea which is so prolific that it is hardly possible to see any leaves among the mass of flowers. Because of this prodigous flowering habit the plant was chosen by the United Nations as a magnificent symbol to link the survival of man with the survival of his environment. Another of this super breed of plants is 'Princess Sonya', a sparkling white variety.

Other particularly lovely azaleas are the red 'Flambeau', 'Lavender Queen', 'Claude Goyet', with its spectacular large dark red double blooms, and the soft pink 'Apple Blossom', 'Blushing Bride' and 'Sherwood's Red'.

Azaleas make excellent cut flowers and will last about five days in water. Cut clusters including both open and unopened buds to ensure continuous flowering. Although you may cut blooms from established azalea bushes, do consider the shape of the bush and prune as you cut.

To condition azaleas split or crush their woody stem ends and leave in cold water overnight. As azaleas love humidity it is wise to spray your arrangement every now and again with a fine mist of cold water as this will encourage buds to open.

STRELITZIA

This exciting indigenous flower is one of those very special species that while not essential, is worth including in your garden if you have the space.

They are not the easiest of flowers to use in arrangements, for they are rather stiff, but there is no doubt that they can look sensational when used properly, particularly in large mixed arrangements. They may also look rather special when used with nothing but their own leaves for decoration.

Were it not for the protea, the strelitzia might well have been our national flower, for its colours are those of our national flag – orange and purple-blue. For this reason they are often used for arrangements on South African stalls at international events.

Also known as the 'Bird of Paradise' plant or the 'Crane flower' because of its strikingly unusual shape, it is one of the easiest plants to cultivate, surviving in almost any position, with sun, shade or neglect. Given plenty of water throughout summer and a little fertilizer before flowering, your strelitzia will be a most rewarding plant.

Strelitzias are slow to establish themselves and hate being moved, but once established they multiply rapidly, growing into lovely rounded clumps which produce dozens and dozens of flowers. These start appearing in April and continue right through winter in areas which do not have severe frost.

Because of their fine rounded shape, clumps of strelitzias make a fine focal point, in rockeries and near pools, where they show to advantage.

A perennial with rhizomatous roots and no stem, its leaves are produced in abundance directly from the base of the plant, giving it an attractive bushy appearance at all times.

The leaves, not unlike Zulu shields, are most attractive and some have a bright pink central vein. These can be curved to suit the arrangement by gently moving your first finger and thumb along either side of the vein to the tip of the leaf in a curving movement. The leaves may be used with all sorts of arrangements throughout the year, either with their own flowers in winter or with others when required.

A strelitzia arrangement will last from two to three weeks; simply top up with water when necessary.

Remember when using strelitzias in

Only a few heads of the crane flowers of the strelitzia are sufficient to make an exciting arrangement but they also make grand displays for special functions in the home, for churches, large halls and hotel lobbies.

massed arrangements that the flowers have little 'faces' which turn in all directions. They, in fact, look less regimented and more natural when facing in a variety of directions in the arrangement.

Because strelitzias, with their long stems, are rather heavy, it is necessary to use a large pin-holder stuck down in your container with Flora Clay or Prestik.

In the accompanying small arrangement three flowers and two buds, together with a number of leaves, were positioned on the pin-holder in a floating bowl. White pebbles were used as a covering to make the arrangement look as natural as possible.

In the very large arrangement, suitable for hallways or receptions rooms, some crumpled 5 cm-gauge chicken wire was used in a terracotta bowl. A flattish container seems to enhance strelitzia arrangements for it enables one to angle flowers more naturally.

South Africa's stunning Bird of Paradise plant (*Strelitzia reginae*), is slow to get going but once it settles down, develops into dense free-flowering bush. Left: Opulent peony blooms.

PEONY

This is another very glamorous plant which is well worth growing if you have the space. For those with cold gardens, who are unable to grow such things as daisies, frangipani and hibiscus, the peony (*Paeonia officinalis*) is a must. As an outstanding cut flower the peony deserves to be better known among arrangers.

Fragrant peonies love the cold and flower best in frosty areas. It is not unknown for gardeners in warmer climates to empty ice trays from the fridge on top of their beloved plants each night throughout the winter in an attempt to give them the degree of chill they enjoy!

These tuberous-rooted plants produce huge ball-like blooms, in single and double forms, displaying some glorious shades of red and purple, the softest blush pink, white and many bi-colours besides. One of the loveliest is a soft sulphur yellow tinged with salmon.

Best planted in light dappled shade or where they get three or four hours of morning sun, peonies need cool, moist soil and should be kept well mulched. Provide a thick layer of well-rotted manure or compost each spring. When planting it is best to trench soil to a depth of about 60 cm and into the top soil work well-rotted kraal manure, a good layer of compost and a fine sprinkling of lime.

Peonies are gross feeders and need a plentiful supply of water and regular feeding with a liquid food.

If planted as tubers peonies will take three years to flower, but today it is possible to buy bagged plants at garden centres. These

bloom immediately and will continue happily in the same position for 20 years or more, producing masses of flowers each spring. In addition to their magnificent blooms they also have beautiful dark, glossy green foliage which is useful for arrangements throughout the summer.

In winter they die down; mark where they are and see they are undisturbed.

Tubers may be divided but are best left alone. If you decide to divide them ensure that each tuber has an eye, which should be set about 5 cm below the surface when planting.

Peonies last in the vase about five days in hot climates and a little longer where cool and are best picked when the buds are half open. Split the ends and keep in cold water overnight. Always cut off old flowers to prevent them draining the plant of nutrients by forming seed unnecessarily.

ABELIA

Of all the flowering shrubs none can be of more use to the flower arranger than the prolific abelia. Not only do they provide enchanting clusters of small flowers, pink or white, but they are most important for their foliage. It is shiny and attractive, often dark green, while the 'Francis Mason' variety offers a beautiful glowing yellow-green leaf. Once these shrubs have grown large enough you can pick freely from their abundant growth, as they quickly put out strong, arching new stems.

In addition to 'Francis Mason', other varieties are 'Edward Goucher', a compact shrub with glossy green leaves and mauve-pink flowers; *A. rupestris*, glossy foliaged with an abundance of tubular pink-tinted white flowers which bloom throughout the summer, and *A. prostrata*, a low-growing plant fine for covering banks as a ground cover. This unusual member of the family has white flowers and spreading branches with shiny green foliage. Its new growth is tinged with red.

Abelia grandiflora.

FRANGIPANI

A tree which grows in many parts of the country – certainly in the warmer areas, the frangipani (*Plumeria rubra*) is so prolific that it can supply a home with cut flowers for many months of the year.

These trees are particularly useful during those hot months, December, January and February, a period when there is often little colour in the garden, and they keep flowering through autumn often until late into May. The handsome leaves of these tropical beauties are also useful for inclusion in arrangements.

The frangipani grows to a size of 4 m x 3 m and produces great heads of fragrant flowers which almost entirely cover it. They have thick succulent branches, which bleed a milky white substance when cut. When picking, flower arrangers should rub the cut ends of flowers in the earth to prevent the exuding sticky substance from messing everything they touch; secateurs will certainly need cleaning after cutting.

The variety of colours now available makes the choice of which frangipani to plant very difficult. They are all beautiful, ranging from ivory to apricot and the deepest burgundy red, but for the flower arranger the common butter-coloured variety and the pale pink are musts.

Frangipani flowers may be floated in bowls or, for a quick arrangement which can be done in under five minutes, use a whole head of flowers surrounded with their own leaves. Such a bowl makes an excellent centre piece for a dinner table. Heads last in water for many days, with buds opening as other flowers fade, and all that is necessary is to remove old blooms. As heads are rather heavy it will be necessary to support them in a stout pincushion.

Frangipani are extremely easy to propagate: cut about 30 cm off the top of any branch, dip in a rooting compound and place in river sand and peat – it will root very quickly. Once planted all it needs to thrive is a warm corner and a reasonable amount of water. Though slow to grow initially, once it gets going it develops beautifully into a great rounded umbrella of a tree which becomes so covered in flowers that you hardly notice the leaves. Feed it once a year with a good mulch of compost and a cupful of SR 3:2:1 (28) and it will give you a great deal of joy for many, many years.

Looking rather like an enormous posy of flowers, frangipani is best viewed from above: plant it beneath a north-facing second storey bedroom window and its fragrance, particularly in the early morning, will give a great deal of pleasure.

Two lovely tropical flowers, those of the frangipani and the coral creeper, provide a stunning decoration for a dinner table when arranged in a shallow bowl.

Common though it may be, the butter-coloured frangipani remains a favourite for floral decoration and is one of the most trouble-free plants you could wish to grow, demanding little but offering beauty all summer long.

101

XI *Through the seasons*

Providing material for the vase throughout the year is easier in South Africa than in most countries of the world because of our generally mild winters, but even here it is necessary to plan well ahead if you are to have flowers and foliage for cutting in all seasons.

Each season has its charms – spring, bursting with bud and the excitement of new growth; summer, voluptuous and bountiful with flower and foliage; autumn, gentle and full of warmth, glowing with leaves like bright embers and winter with its stark beauty.

WINTER

Only winter holds any real problems for the arranger, testing your skill as a gardener, but even during this period it is possible, with careful husbandry, to grow sufficient for the vase to see you through the cold months.

It is now that your diary plays an important role. Take careful note of when certain plants bloom and berry, of which foliage is looking good, which grasses have dried attractively, even of which twigs have charm and which dead fronds and fading foliage will add interest to your arrangements.

For the first few seasons you might miss out occasionally but once you have lived through a few winters in your garden and also checked those of friends and neighbours, you should have no problems.

Although colour is often difficult to obtain in winter, it is nonetheless possible to find flowers that bloom in every month of the year and I have added some lists to the end of the chapter to assist the arranger. These suggestions are general, however, and you may find that in your particular area you are able to grow more, while gardeners in other areas may find the plants mentioned unsuitable.

It is very much a matter of experimentation so don't be afraid to try tender plants

In the depths of winter, when flowers are hard to come by, potted cyclamen come to the rescue. Groups of these – particularly the mini variety – look beautiful when grouped in a 'vase' and last for many weeks.

Japanese flowering quince is one of the most useful of all winter standbys. It flowers in many areas from as early as June, on into spring. For arrangements it is ideal, making striking displays whether used alone or in combination with other plants. It is particularly useful for stark Ikebana arrangements.

in sheltered spots – it is surprising what some people are able to grow in what might seem an unlikely area because of a particular mini climate prevailing in their garden. A neighbour of mine has two huge poinsettia bushes in her garden and every year one of them has its flowers burned by the frost while the other, not 15 metres away, but cuddled by some tall neighbouring trees, blooms magnificently.

The colder your area, the more difficult to propagate flowering plants, but there are some, such as camellias, which are perfectly hardy and provide not only magnificent blooms but also excellent foliage.

Probably the most rewarding of all winter flowering shrubs is the Japanese quince (*Chaenomeles lagenaria*), a plant which grows rather slowly to about 2 m x 2 m in size. Not only does it produce a mass of flowers for nearly two months at a time, but also has fascinating foliage – bright apple-green when young and later tinted purple at the edges. Finally it produces attractive fruit which remain on the branches for a long time.

The colour of its flowers varies from pure white (*Maulei nivalis*) to shell pink (*Moerloesii*), orange-scarlet (*Umblicata rubra*) and salmon-orange ('Falconet Charlet'), plus a dwarf variety with dark red flowers and yellow stamens ('Crimson and Gold'). As interesting as its flowers are the fascinating angular shapes of its stems. The oddly formed and bent branches make quinces particularly good picking material for arrangements – especially when used on their own for Ikebana designs. If picked while still in tight bud, flowers will open over a long period, with arrangements lasting two weeks or more – even in shallow bowls, as long as they are topped up regularly.

Also useful for winter colour is our indigenous strelitzia which starts blooming as early as April. In frost-free areas it continues producing its lovely crane-like blooms well into winter.

Although the strelitzia seen in most gardens is the striking orange and purple plant, there are indeed other varieties. Shades range from yellow, through apricot to the brilliance of the common variety. All of them are worth having if possible.

In most places arum lilies and winter flowering red hot pokers will put on a show. Snapdragons are marvellous cut flowers for late winter, as are Iceland poppies, sweet peas, calendulas, pansies and the little English daisy.

Early flowering poppies provide cut flowers in late winter.

Daisies of most kinds are a good bet in winter, with marguerites flourishing in all but the coldest areas. If they don't get frosted in your region, it is wise to grow as many varieties as possible: single and double pinks, including the gorgeous Ruby Red, the many varieties of white and certainly the yellows.

One of the highlights of late winter is the advent of the lovely Chinese jasmine (*J. polyanthum*), which always heralds the approaching spring by scenting the garden with its fragrance and adding dazzling splashes of white to bleak backgrounds. With its tight pink buds and white starry flowers, the jasmine is also a delight in the home, trailing out of mixed bowls or providing opulent displays on its own.

Grown in pots or beds, cineraria and primulas provide other bright spots for dull days and continue flowering well into the spring. They produce some glorious clear colours for lightening indoor arrangements – pale pinks and lilacs, reds and purples of the dainty primulas and the lovely soft blues and beiges, browns, purples and wine colours of the cinerarias.

Indoor arrangements need not only be made with cut flowers. An excellent idea is to grow pot plants such as cyclamen or a few bulb varieties such as daffodils (*Narcissus*), hyacinths and tulips. These look good either alone or mixed with other pot plants in living arrangements. It is useful to keep a variety of good colourful indoor plants, such as the bushy dieffenbachia, 'Rudolph Roehrs', with its lovely lemon-green colouring, the various aglaonemas, peperomias, marantas, as well as some ferns which may be mixed to make attractive and colourful arrangements.

Quite popular today is the designing of *pot-et-fleur*, a method of arranging growing plants with cut flowers, or perhaps even driftwood and stones. It can be very effective, but the busy housewife or career woman would probably do better to stick to one-plant groupings, such as five small pots of cyclamen. These may be either one colour or mixed, and once arranged will last for many weeks. It is necessary only to keep the plants watered and to remove dead heads. If you feel the group needs a little something extra, try including some trailing asparagus, a few fronds of ivy or a tendril or two of periwinkle.

Although blossoms are associated with spring, it is well to remember that in late winter it is often possible, in our warmer areas, to introduce a breath of spring by producing blossoms from bare but budded branches of peaches, plums and crab-apples. This is done by plunging the branches into containers of warm water which, if kept in a warm room, will cause the buds to open in a fine early display.

Ikebana fundis are particularly clever with their winter arrangements and it is well worth while attending exhibitions to collect ideas for your arrangements and to learn from the experts' clever use of varied materials. Study the material used during winter and how it is used – the art has been developed over centuries. (*See also Ikebana chapter*).

The busy little yellow marguerite flowers thoughout the year providing masses of flowers for the vase even in winter.

SPRING

Spring is a time when you can be tempted to overdo your arrangements. Thus it is wise to make bold one-flower arrangements, for what could look nicer than a beautiful vaseful of tulips or daffodils, sweet peas or irises? But, if you feel like going overboard with an outrageous mixed bowl, no one will blame you for a dose of spring fever – flowers can never look vulgar, no matter how many you put together. They can look messy, however, so be careful – don't throw overboard the basic principles of good design.

Spring is a time for colour, particularly as many bulbs flower at this time – ranunculus, anemones, freesias, daffodils, tulips and hyacinths. In addition there are masses of annuals, bountiful blossoms, some of the perennials and many of the shrubs and climbers that put on their biggest show in August, September and October.

At this time of year there is so much you want to plant that it is a good opportunity to overplant bulbs with annuals, so enjoying two crops in the space of one. There are a great many combinations worth trying: lavender primulas with daffodils; white or yellow Dutch irises with blue lobelia; blue violas with yellow treated tulips, and fragrant freesias with red pansies – flower arrangers will dream up dozens more to suit their particular schemes.

There was a time when violas were chosen in preference to pansies for their lovely bright, clear colours, but in recent years pansies have been hybridized in such a way that they are rapidly taking over the role of violas for striking single-colour beds. Today it is possible to find beautiful red, white and blue pansies, as well as yellows, and not only are their flowers bigger and brighter but they are less temperamental and

more floriferous. They also make far better cut flowers.

Namaqualand daisies are not normally thought of as cut flowers because they close as the sun goes down, but they do in fact make enchanting small displays for sunny windowsills. They are ideal for rooms which are used only during the day such as the kitchen or sewing room, but can be used anywhere for they are attractive even in repose. They will provide a lively arrangement which may last for five or six days.

Flowering early in spring, Namaqualands, or African daisies as they are often called, offer breathtaking garden vistas when planted en masse. Snowdrifts of the glistening white variety are sensational when planted alone in pockets or tumbling over banks.

Namaqualands are easy to grow but many people make the mistake of sowing seed too early. This should not be done before April (preferably early May for best results), for should there be late summer rains they often get too wet and the seeds rot. Planting early achieves nothing; they will still flower at their appointed time.

Prepare for sowing by cultivating the soil to a depth of about 15 cm and cover the entire area with a 3 cm thick layer of compost. Work the soil over well. Seed should be sown *in situ* and spread as evenly as possible. Rake lightly and water just enough to moisten the soil.

Keep the soil damp until plants are rooted, then reduce watering, for in nature they are accustomed to very dry conditions and are inclined to damp off.

Marguerites are of course flowering at this time – as they do for many other months of the year. Do not overlook them, for they mix well with many of the other spring flowers, and the yellow varieties look particularly good mixed with lively blue Forget-me-nots.

Queen Anne's lace, that long flowering delight which is too rarely seen in gardens these days, is another beauty which comes into its own at this time of year. It can be included successfully with a great variety of flowers, softening the brash and lightening the bold. After picking Queen Anne's lace, be sure to strip off the leaves and plunge the stems into 5 cm boiling water for five minutes.

Behold – a host of golden daffodils.

Cut tulips with their attractive stems look superb in clear glass vases. Arranging tulips in such a way is easy – but don't expect them to stay the way you placed them, they invariably rearrange themselves.

A celebration of spring — two glorious mixed bowls. Choice of material is a matter of taste and what you have available in the garden — anything goes.

From spring onwards through summer the mixed bowl, considered by many as the most charming of all vase decorations, comes into its own and with this type of arrangement virtually anything goes. The choice of material is a matter of taste and what you have in your garden.

The mixed arrangement may be of any size, but is more often than not a substantial affair for the centre of the dining-room table, an altar arrangement in church, for a sideboard or for a mantlepiece backed by a large mirror which lends depth to the decoration.

In spring there are few mixed bowls which do not include some blossom, for these lovely flowers are very much a symbol of the season. Many gardeners think of them as transitory, but a Pretoria friend who adores them has arranged her garden so that she has some variety of blossom available for the vase from July until October. In colder and warmer areas the following periods may vary slightly but will give a rough guide. Following the calendar from July she has many flowering quinces of different colours and these provide pickings for three months. In addition there are:

• A number of prunus varieties. These lovely trees, which flower through August and September are noted both for their flowers in spring and their foliage – particu-

Daffodils, used with their own foliage make a simple but charming display.

Bright ranunculus add colour to the garden and home and joy of joys, they flower the better for being dead-headed.

larly the flowering plums with their purple and tinted leaves – for most of the year.

• Several flowering ornamental peach varieties are useful for flower arrangers, plus the miniature which is ideal for the town-house or small garden. Its entire spread is only a matter of 1,5 m and in addition to flowers it bears Jubilee-type fruit which ripens at Christmas time. 'Saturn' is another dream variety which keeps both the arrangers and the fruit lovers in the family happy, being the first 'flowering' peach which bears not only gorgeous double pink blossoms but also luscious Jubilee-type fruit in December.

• Following the prunus varieties come the cherries, which flourish at the end of September and on into October.

• Also flowering at various times between August and October are the many spectacularly beautiful crab-apples (*Malus* varieties) which vary in colour from white and pale pink to reds and combinations of these colours. Some of them also offer a bonus of attractive foliage and fruits which are useful in flower designs.

As do most flowering fruit trees, these all thrive particularly well in colder areas, such as the Free State – where the cherries are in their element – and on the chilly Highveld, where blossoms last much longer than in the warmer regions.

For flower arranging with blossoms, the best time of day for picking is early in the morning when buds are just opening. Stem ends should be split and then plunged into deep water and left to soak for several hours. Blossoms are particularly thirsty and vases need to be topped up regularly. You may find that double cherry blossoms do not open well if cut at the bud stage, they often need to be left until about two-thirds open.

Another tip for making blossom last in the vase is to put a tablespoon of sugar into the water; flowers will last four to five days in all but the hottest weather.

Mixed Namaqualand daisies ideal for sunny windowsills.

Massed in the sun, white Namaqualand daisies form glistening 'snowdrifts'.

110

Primulas – one of the joys of spring for garden and vase.

Primulas today come in a great variety of shades, from white and soft pink and lilac to deep purple, even red. Here some of the shades are beautifully blended and superbly complemented by silver accessories.

SUMMER

Summer is a season for perennials and a time when you can enjoy the continuing rose season which started with a blaze in October and which will continue until winter. Lilies of various kinds come into their own, as do cannas, gladioli and watsonias. Summer annuals are also at the peak of their glory. Remember that unless you have planned your garden well, Christmas time is often a barren period and you should take advantage of such free flowering delights as hydrangeas, hibiscus and frangipani.

Easy to grow liliums are underrated plants in South Africa and deserve to be better known. Not only do they provide colour throughout the summer but are most useful plants for home decoration. Rarely troubled by pests or diseases and requiring only a minimum of attention, they are versatile and can be used successfully in beds, borders or pots.

Many lilies have the added attraction of being fragrant, with the stunning tall St Joseph *(L. longiflorum)* a wonderful example. Not only do these blooms scent the garden, but just one included in a flower arrangement or bridal bouquet can be a real delight.

Although summer flowering, bulbs of these beautiful plants become available in nurseries and garden centres during May and June and should be planted as soon after purchase as possible. Lilies only show above ground in the spring, but don't be fooled by the fact that they take up to four months to appear. During the winter the bulb grows an elaborate root system and it is only when this has fully developed that shoots will appear above ground.

When planting it is wise to dig over your bed to a depth of about 45 cm, ensuring that there is good drainage – even by placing river sand or small stones at the bottom of each bulb hole. Lilies are lovers of rich compost and this should be spread thickly over the bed. Add also a handful of bonemeal for each square metre of bed; if this is done properly there will be no need for any other fertilizer.

Once planted, the soil above the bulbs should be covered with a mulch, preferably peat moss, to keep the soil cool and moist.

It is best to position lilies where they get

Two striking yellow lilium varieties are: (above) L. 'Connecticut King' and (below) the free flowering 'Yellow Tiger'.

The spotted, orange Tiger lily remains one of the all-time favourites among lilium growers.

some morning sun and good light but NO afternoon sun. They are happiest when their roots are shaded by other plants, but their heads are able to grow into the light. If planted in an open bed it is wise to overplant with annuals such as dwarf marigolds, candytuft or the small snapdragons. In partial shade, lilies are very effective grown through graceful columbines, foxgloves or ferns.

Watering of lilies is important and varies from winter to summer. During the cold months they enjoy a good soaking once every 10 days. Once growth appears above ground step up the rate to every five days. Unlike most other bulbous species the lilium never has a dormant period; almost immediately stems have died down new shoots begin to form in the bulb.

Once flowering is over, reduce watering but do not stop entirely for it is important that the plants continue to grow, mature and prepare themselves for another season's blooming. It is at this time of year that you should feed bulbs with a good organic liquid fertilizer to boost them for the following summer's flowering.

An important point here is that stems should not be cut off at the end of the flowering season. The bulbs need their stems to provide them with food for the following year's growth. Once stems are dead, however, they may be cut off just above the soil level.

When buying bulbs ensure they are sound and crisp with no soft spots. Do not worry about size, for large or small they will still produce good plants and flowers.

There are many liliums available in South Africa, ranging from 50 cm to 200 cm in height, and which bloom from September well into the following year.

For a good display which will last for several months, you might for instance start with the 50 cm tall varieties: *L. umbellatum* (red) and *L.* 'Day Spring' (yellow) for flowering in September and October. These could be followed by that ever cheerful *L.* 'Golden Souvenir', which grows to about one metre and flowers through October and November.

Then for November-December extending into the new year, try some of the tall growing varieties (from 1 m to 2 m) such as *L.* 'Pink Perfection', the white St Joseph (*L. longiflorum*), *L.* 'Golden Trumpets' and the orange favourite, Tiger lily (*L. tigrinum splendens*).

Lily bulbs are best left in the ground for at least three years before separating and they may well be left for much longer.

Summer is a time for flowering herbs and the umbels of many of these are extremely useful in arrangements. A useful example is the yarrow (*Achillea*) which not only flourishes throughout the warm months, but finally dries on the bush and is useful for fine autumn displays.

Scented St Joseph lilies, one of the joys of the summer garden.

Lilium sutari (right) is another spotted orange lilium but has much larger blooms than the tiger. It is an excellent cut flower.

114

AUTUMN

Autumn is a most exciting season for the arranger. In addition to the many flowers which are still available, there is also the marvellous coloured foliage which is useful for exciting and unusual displays.

One of the outstanding flowers of autumn is the Japanese anemone with its lovely white, pink and double pink blooms, lasting many weeks through late March and April. Not to be overlooked are the montbretias, Michaelmas daisies, dahlias and delphiniums, as well as those ever reliable roses, with some such as 'Iceberg', 'Freesia' and 'Queen Elizabeth' hardly taking a rest.

Other autumn delights are the nerines, those striking indigenous plants which, despite being one of the best cut flowers available, are rarely seen even in arrangers' gardens. Members of the amaryllis family, nerines, bear their clusters of lovely crimped ribbon-like blooms at the top of 25 cm to 30 cm-long, slender but strong stems. Their closely packed clusters of six to eight blooms are a delight and most decorative in single flower or mixed bowl arrangements.

Very new on the market in South Africa are the vari-coloured nerines and the best news for gardeners is that they are now not only available as cut flowers in florist's shops but also available as bulbs in nurseries and garden centres.

While the original nerine (*N. sarniensis*), often mistakenly called the Guernsey lily, produces only one flower stem every second season, these new hybrids produce two stems every year – making them more than worthwhile in the arranger's garden. The new varieties available include a gorgeous salmon, with the rather fun name of 'Serendipity'; a dark pink ('Pink Sensation'), a light pink ('Baby Doll') and a vivid red ('Prima Ballerina').

Mr Floris Barnhoorn, of Hadeco, the South African bulb growers who introduced these nerines into South Africa, says that a white nerine is also being developed at the moment and he is hopeful that it will be available to the gardener within a few years. Although a white nerine has been discovered by botanists at Kirstenbosch, this natural variety, while of interest to collectors, is not as floriferous as the hybrid strains.

The most exciting new bulb now on the market and available to gardeners is a spec-

Newly available to South African gardeners, the fabulous hybrid nerines promise to become one of the musts in any arranger's garden. The four new colours are: light pink 'Baby Doll', dark pink 'Pink Sensation', salmon pink 'Serendipity' and bright red 'Prima Ballerina'.

The recently introduced pink Amarina 'Zwanenburg' is a cross between a nerine and an Amaryllis belladonna and produces large flower heads on 60 cm to 70 cm tall stems.

tacular world first for South Africa – the Amarine 'Zwanenburg'. It is a gorgeous cyclamen pink beauty which grows on stems 70 cm tall bearing flower umbels rather like those of a nerine although much larger. This lovely 'first' is in fact a cross between the nerine and another South African beauty, the *Amaryllis belladonna*, and bears the best characteristics of both parents.

Both the nerines and the amarine are easy to grow given their requirements. They do best in a sandy, well drained soil and are perfect for rockeries. They should be planted with the tops of the bulbs barely covered. Clumps of nerines may be left for four or five years before division is necessary.

The new hybrid nerines will be available in shops during November each year and may be planted in November, December or January for autumn flowering, with the first flowering in March, continuing for three weeks.

After flowering at the end of autumn leaves continue to develop and liquid food should be provided to build them up for their next flowering period. Cease watering however, once the leaves start turning yellow and dying down. Nerines require a period of dormancy during which time they should be kept dry.

Autumn is a time for the oranges and golds, coppers, reds and bronzes and most of these colours can be provided by berries, including the *Pyracantha* 'Orange Charmer', cotoneasters, hawthorns and the many deciduous trees which put on a spectacular display before their bright leaves are scattered by raw winds.

AUTUMN FOLIAGE

Many South Africans are fanatical cultivators of evergreen trees, possibly out of fear of leaves falling in swimming pools, but there is no doubt that the really interesting trees are those that add fire and colour to the garden scene before shedding their 'crowning glory'. These are also, to a large extent, the most valuable for the flower arranger.

There are many areas in the garden where deciduous trees are most important. One of these is in front of that north-facing master bedroom, where shade is needed to keep it cool in summer but which should allow in sun, light and warmth in winter.

Other important places are patio and braai areas as evergreens grown in these positions cut out the use of these areas in winter.

There are many fine deciduous trees that could be used for such positions but for the arranger useful choices include the maples, such as *Acer trifidium*, a smallish tree which turns a brilliant red in autumn; *A. negundo*, the box elder maple, which has an ash-like appearance and which turns bright yellow in autumn and the ghost tree (*A. negundo* 'Argenteum Variegatum'), which has highly

Autumn foliage provides an abundance of material for the flower arranger and here a wide variety has been used to produce a sensational colour arrangement in a large copper jug, without including a single flower.
  Material used: (1) *Prunus nigra*; (2) Pride of India; (3) berberis; (4) Virginia creeper; (5) pomegranate; (6) Japanese Heavenly bamboo; (7) trailing stems of variegated honeysuckle and (8) lemons and (9) a small branch of yellowing gardenia leaves.

'Orange Charmer' is an excellent name for this bright *Pyracantha*.

Snippets of pyracantha make wonderful tubby little arrangements.

Basketware and cane complement red hawthorn and the orange berries of the Pyracantha, a striking decoration for a patio.

BERRIES

Each season produces its own special beauties in the garden – but none more striking than the spectacular berries that herald autumn, hedges laden with those 'monkey apples' that remind most of us of happy childhood days.

Berry bushes are a vital part of the flower arranger's garden and it is worth growing as large a variety as possible. Among the most useful are the hawthorns and the cotoneasters – even groundcover varieties being available for small gardens. Not only do they provide berries but are covered during summer in sprays of small white, honey-scented, flowers and attractive foliage.

Easy to grow and totally undemanding once established, the various berry bushes are singularly free of disease and other problems.

Little treatment is needed when preparing berry branches for arrangements other than to remove the lower thorns and leaves and to crush or slit their stout stems.

Lasting up to 10 days in the vase if the water is topped up regularly, they look good alone, blended with other coloured berries or in mixed arrangements. Berries also show up well in foliage designs. They are very adaptable for it is possible to cut either long lengths for large arrangements or mere snippets for small ones.

A variety of containers will complement berry arrangements from rough textured baskets to dull surfaced ceramics and even fine porcelains, and are particularly handsome in brass and copper.

A delight in summer, the Pride of India (*Lagerstroemia indica*) (left) also offers one of the most beautiful autumn displays with leaves turning to yellow, orange, red and gold, before exposing their attractive grey stems in winter (below).

The autumn leaves of the Virginia creeper covering a jacaranda tree provide a brightly patterned canopy.

Rhus succedanea (bottom right) produces spectacular autumn shadings on some parts of the tree while others remain green.

ornamental variegated silver-cream foliage in summer in addition to its autumn shadings. One of the real delights of the maples is that they are of a size which may be conveniently used by townhouse and small-plot gardeners.

Another brilliant specimen is the popular Liquid Amber (*L. styraciflua*) whose leaves resemble molten lava during its glowing autumn display.

The wax tree, a member of the *Rhus* family (*R. succedanea*), is a glory in autumn, with its glossy leaves turning to shades of orange and finally a brilliant scarlet.

Then there's that granddaddy of trees – the maidenhair tree (*Ginkgo biloba*). Rarely growing taller than 12 m with a 6 m spread, its fern-like leaves turn to a rich butter yellow in autumn. These trees are considered living fossils, their origins dating back to pre-history.

A very showy shrub which produces masses of flowers during summer is the Pride of India (*Lagerstroemia indica*) available in a variety of colours including pale pink, rose, lilac, mauve, red and white – but it is its autumn leaves rather than its flowers which really interest the arranger. Few plants have lovelier fall foliage, the Pride of India glowing with rich reds, golds and yellows before shedding its leaves to reveal attractive pale grey stems.

For cold areas an ideal plant is the persimmon (*Diospyros kaki*). This charming small Eastern tree not only produces glorious shiny foliage which colours magnificently in autumn, but is never more lovely than when the leaves disappear in early winter and it is left starkly displaying its striking red-orange fruits on bare stems.

Autumn is not only a time for glowing foliage, there are also many beautiful flowers available in gardens, as shown in this Victorian posy, displaying a variety of coloured single chrysanthemums, roses, carnations and gypsophila.

Large mixed arrangements are ideal for reception rooms, functions and church displays – just right for the grand occasion. Here we see massed chrysanthemums of different colours.

Flowers available for picking for the vase during the twelve months of the year:

JANUARY

Ageratum
Alyssum
Amaranthus
Amaryllis
Arum (golden, pink, white)
Aster
Begonia (tuberose)
Bougainvillea
Browallia
Calliopsis
Candytuft
Canna
Carnation
Celosia
Chrysanthemum
Cleome
Columbine
Dahlia
Daisy varieties (Marguerites)
Delphinium elatum
Delphinium sinensis
Dianthus
Everlasting (*Helichrysum*)
Foxglove
Frangipani
Gaillardia
Galtonia
Gardenia
Geranium
Gladiolus
Gloriosa daisy
Golden rod (*Solidago canadensis*)
Gypsophila
Hollyhock
Hibiscus varieties
Hydrangea
Impatiens
Lavatera trimestris
Liatris
Lilium varieties
Linaria
Lobelia
Marigold
Matricaria
Monkey plant (*Mimulus cupreus*)
Nasturtium
Nierembergia
Nikki (*Nicotiana*)
Pansy
Penstemon
Petunia
Phlox
Rose
Salvia varieties
Snapdragon
Sweet William
Watsonia
Zinnia

FEBRUARY

Ageratum
Alyssum
Arum (golden, pink, white)
Aster
Begonia (tuberous)
Canna
Dahlia
Daisy varieties (Marguerites)
Delphinium elatum
Delphinium sinensis
Dianthus
Frangipani
Fuchsia
Gloriosa daisy
Golden rod (*Solidago canadensis*)
Gypsophila
Hibiscus
Hydrangea
Japanese anemone
Lavatera trimestris
Lilium varieties
Lobelia
Marigold
Matricaria
Nerine
Nicotiana
Penstemon
Petunia
Phlox
Rose
Salvia varieties
Shasta daisy
Snapdragon
Sweet William
Watsonia
Zinnia

MARCH

Ageratum
Alyssum
Arum (white)
Begonia (tuberous)
Canna
Chilli (*Solanum* varieties)
Chincherinchee
Coleus
Dahlia
Daisy varieties (Marguerites)
Frangipani
Fuchsia
Geranium
Gladiolus
Hibiscus
Japanese anemone
Linaria
Lobelia
Marigold
Monbretia
Nasturtium
Nerine

Nicotiana
Petunia
Phlox
Rose
Snapdragon
Verbena
Zinnia

APRIL

Alyssum
Arum (white)
Camellia sasanqua
Chilli (*Solanum* varieties)
Dahlia
Daisy varieties (Marguerites)
Frangipani
Gladiolus
Gloxinia
Hibiscus
Lobelia
Nerine
Nikki (if cut back earlier)
Petunia
Phlox
Rose
Snapdragon

MAY

Alyssum
Arum (white)
Camellia
Daisy varieties (Marguerites)
Hibiscus
Gloxinia
Lobelia
Petunia
Phlox
Rose
Snapdragon

JUNE

Alyssum
Arum (white)
Calendula
Camellia
Daisy varieties (Marguerites)
English daisy (*Bellis perennis*)
Lobelia
Magnolia
Petunia
Phlox
Rose
Primula malacoides
Snapdragon

JULY

Allium
Alyssum
Anemone

Many of the prunus varieties provide both flowers and beautiful bronze-coloured foliage for the vase.

Arum (white)
Azalea
Calendula
Camellia
Daffodil (treated)
Daisy varieties (Marguerites)
English daisy
Hyacinth
Iceland poppy
Iris (Dutch)
Lobelia
Japanese flowering quince
Jasmine
Magnolia
Nemesia
Pansy
Petunia
Phlox
Primula malacoides
Primula veris
Ranunculus
Schizanthus
Snapdragon
Stocks
Sweet pea
Tulip (treated)
Viola

The heavy flowers were balanced in the bowl but the arrangement was also braced by the statuette. If necessary it is always possible to give a vase extra support, if you fear it is going to topple, by sticking it to the table with easy-to-remove florist's clay.

For the photograph, the arrangement was placed on a silver tray on a coffee table but would have looked equally well against a wall of a lounge or reception room.

For special occasions statues may be included with flowers to great advantage and this arrangement to celebrate 'The Year of the Child' is a lovely example. Heavy branches of soft pink peach blossom were used as a foil for the pink-grey of the statue. The arrangement itself was done in a cheap plastic florist's bowl, about 15 cm in diameter which was filled with oasis, bound into the vase with florist's tape.

AUGUST

Allium
Alyssum
Anemone
Arum (white)
Azalea
Calendula
Daisy varieties (Marguerites)
Daffodil (treated)
English daisy (*Bellis perennis*)
Grape hyacinth (*Muscari*)
Freesia
Hyacinth
Iris (Dutch)
Lachenalia
Lavatera trimestris
Lobelia
Japanese Flowering Quince
Namaqualand daisy
Nemesia
Pansy
Petunia
Phlox
Poppy
Primula malacoides
Primula veris
Ranunculus
Schizanthus

Scilla
Snowflakes (*Leucojum*)
Stock
Sweet pea
Tea bush (*Leptospermum*)
Tulip (treated)

SEPTEMBER

Ageratum
Allium
Alyssum
Amaryllis
Anemone
Arum (white)
Bluebell (*Endymion*)
Calendula
Canterbury bell
Columbine
Crocus
Daffodil
Daisy varieties (*Marguerites*)
Freesia
Grape hyacinth (*Muscari*)
Iris (bearded)
Iris (Dutch)
Ixia
Lachenalia
Lavatera trimestris
Leucojum
Lilium varieties
Marigold
Matricaria
Namaqualand daisy
Nemesia
Pansy
Peony
Petunia
Phlox
Poppy
Primula malacoides
Primula veris
Ranunculus
Schizanthus
Scilla
Snowflakes (*Leucojum*)
Sparaxis
Stock
Sweet pea
Tea bush (*Leptospermum*)
Tritonia
Tulip
Viola
Watsonia (white)

OCTOBER

Ageratum
Alyssum
Amaryllis
Arum (white)
Azalea
Babiana

Calendula
Canterbury bell
Chlidanthus
Chincherinchee (*Ornithogalum*)
Daisy varieties (Marguerites)
Gladiolus
Hibiscus
Iris (Dutch)
Iris (bearded)
Ixia
Lavatera trimestris
Lilium (*L. umbellatum* varieties)
Lobelia
Marigold
Matricaria
Pansy
Peony
Petunia
Phlox
Poppy
Ranunculus
Rose
Snapdragon
Sweet pea
Tritonia
Viola
Watsonia

NOVEMBER

Ageratum
Alyssum
Amaryllis
Arum (golden, pink, green, white)
Aster
Canterbury bell
Canna
Carnation
Chlidanthus
Cleome
Columbine
Dahlia
Daisy varieties (Marguerites)
Delphinium elatum
Delphinium sinensis
Dianthus
Foxglove
Fuchsia
Gardenia
Gladiolus
Gloriosa daisy
Golden rod (*Solidago canadensis*)
Gypsophila
Hibiscus
Hydrangea
Iris (Louisiana)
Lilium
Lobelia
Marigold
Matricaria
Nicotiana
Pansy
Penstemon

Petunia
Phlox
Rose
Snapdragon
Sprekelia
Sweet William
Tigridia
Tuberose (*Polianthus*)
Verbena
Zinnia

DECEMBER

Agapanthus
Ageratum
Alyssum
Amaryllis
Arum (golden, pink, white, green)
Aster
Canna
Carnation
Canterbury bell
Cleome
Clematis
Columbine
Dahlia
Daisy varieties (Marguerites)
Delphinium elatum
Delphinium sinensis
Dianthus
Eucomis
Foxglove
Frangipani
Fuchsia
Galtonia
Gardenia
Gladiolus
Gloriosa daisy
Golden rod
Gypsophila
Hibiscus
Hydrangea
Iris (*Kaempferi*)
Lavatera trimestris
Liatris
Lilium
Lobelia
Marigold
Matricaria
Nicotiana
Pansy
Penstemon
Petunia
Phlox
Rose
Salvia varieties
Snapdragon
Sprekelia
Sweet William
Tigridia
Verbena
Watsonia
Zinnia

XII *Flowers for the occasion*

Flowers and foliage have been associated with festivals and special occasions since earliest times. Today it is almost unthinkable to contemplate a baptism or marriage, a golden wedding or a barmitzvah without flowers. No dinner party is complete without blooms decorating the table, and Christmas would not be Christmas without holly and ivy and flowers of some kind. Who could imagine a national event without arrangements of strelitzia and protea, or a church service without flowers?

Dates of most special occasions are usually known well in advance, which means that one is able to plan one's garden and floral decorations to suit such events as a golden wedding or a 21st birthday party – even years in advance if necessary.

Even brides wanting to use the home garden for their wedding receptions are generally considerate enough to give parents sufficient advance notice to enable them to plant special beds and colour combinations for wedding-breakfast tables and decorations for the church. But even if an event is sprung on you, there is generally enough in the arranger's garden to produce reasonable decorations. Even if you have to buy some special coloured material from florist or flower seller at the time, a well maintained garden will contain all the background and filler material you will need.

For anyone planning an occasion in advance, the colour lists at the end of Chapter IX and the month by month lists at the end of Chapter XI will prove useful.

Among the most regular of special occasions is the home dinner party and for these you can simply use what is available in the garden at the particular time of year. A word of warning here, however – avoid using fragrant flowers at the dinner table, particularly anything with a very strong scent such as Chinese jasmine. You will not want to nauseate your guests with a plant's penetrating perfume or overwhelm the ap-

petizing smells of roast lamb or the delicate fragrance of a subtly herbed sauce.

It is worth remembering that fruit is as useful as flowers for table arrangements, giving your decor an opulent look. At a time when there are no flowers in the garden, fruit decorations may be 'dollied up' by the inclusion of foliage such as ivy or asparagus.

For an important occasion buy a few special flowers, perhaps even an orchid, to include in your arrangement. Often by doing this you are able to add a touch of luxury to what may otherwise have been a very ordinary design.

Flowers are a major part of the Christmas scene and no festive table is complete without a beautiful floral centrepiece.

'The ham,' you protest, 'and the turkey, not to mention the cookies – how can I manage flowers, too?' Well, there are a number of easy-to-prepare, simple but delightful arrangements which may be done quickly, using flowers available at that time. All you need are hydrangeas, roses, hibiscus, geraniums and carnations – flowers that

are generally available in most gardens at Christmas time.

Although Christmas is undoubtedly the main festival of the year, there are many other occasions on which you will want flowers.

Easter is often a time for visitors and flowers will brighten the home. A perfect Easter flower that comes to mind, certainly for those living in the northern provinces, is cosmos. Fields are so bright and beautiful with these charming flowers at this time of year that they could almost be considered a symbol of Easter. Because they enliven the autumn veld with splashes of white, soft pinks and bold burgundies, one is inclined to think of them as wild flowers. In fact, they are wonderful candidates for the garden, with cultivated varieties even coming in yellow and orange. Proof of the

This mass of cosmos colour was photographed along a Transvaal roadside but it is possible to create an equally attractive display in your garden. Easy to grow, these tall annuals are ideal on banks or at the back of sunny borders.

There is no end to the variety of arrangements possible for special occasions and they can be sensational without being extravagant in the way of flowers. This one required little time or material. Champagne for two was the theme and a single rose and ribbons plus beautifully packaged gifts were all that were necessary to set a cosy scene.

ease with which they can be grown is seen in the way they seed themselves and flourish in the veld.

Sun is their greatest need, for they are undemanding of soil or water. They are an ideal choice for the back of borders as they grow to a metre or more in height and flower over a long period. For the vase they provide a variety of single and double flowers, often up to 10 cm across, and their fine lacy foliage lends an airy quality to an arrangement.

The many-flowered umbels of 'Apple Blossom' Dombeya, a floriferous indigenous shrub, make excellent arrangements for a variety of situations, from bridal bouquets to simple church or home arrangements.

Their lovely palette of colours makes them ideal flowers for single variety arrangements, but it is also a charming idea to mix them with a few heads of tall grass or perhaps some wild statice to give them a wonderfully natural feel of the veld.

Also flowering at around Easter time is a rather showy indigenous shrub worth a place in all but the smallest of gardens – the Apple Blossom Dombeya (*D. burgessiae*) which grows to about 3m x 3m and displays lovely white flowers tinged with pink. Not only are these flowers useful in fresh arrangements but they also dry very well. The bloom of dombeya varieties is carried in many-flowered umbels, either round or flat, varying in colour from pink to white. Fresh

or dried they make excellent small posy-like arrangements ideal for Easter brides or as table decorations.

Different varieties of dombeya are indigenous to different parts of Southern Africa and all of them are beautiful. *D. dregeana* is found all over Natal, along the south coast into Transkei and as far south as Port Elizabeth, while *D. rotundifolia* is to be found from the northern part of Natal, through the Eastern Transvaal and up into Central Africa.

Dombeyas form rounded shrubs or small trees and do well in poor soil, tolerating not only light frost but also a fair amount of drought. They are quick growing in the warmer parts of the country.

There are often special occasions when flowers of a certain colour are required – pinks and blues for births and whites for weddings – and these most gardens have anyway, but less readily available are blooms for a golden or silver wedding. Such celebrations are best prepared for well in advance, as certain times of the year might prove tricky.

For golden weddings there are many yellow flowers available at most times of the year – yellow marguerites are available all year round – but when it comes to real gold there are two gorgeous flowers which come to mind. The first is the hibiscus 'Full Moon', which has a glorious form and colour, and the second, so aptly named Golden rod (*Solidago canadensis*). Both flower for long periods during summer.

Golden rod is a true gold and the modern hybrids produce their bold sprays of bloom from late November through to autumn. Growing to about a metre tall, they are most striking when grouped in borders.

Silver is a more difficult colour to obtain and white is usually used while there are no silver flowers. It is here that foliage comes into its own. There are a number of plants which are extremely useful, such as the Cape silver tree, Lamb's ears (*Stachys lenata*), as well as some of the herbs, including santolina and wormwood (*Artemesia*) and the large leaves of the globe artichoke. Particularly useful on such occasions are the silvery seedpods of Honesty (*Lunaria*) and branches of the penny gum (*Eucalyptus cinerea*).

Although it could hardly be called a true silver the closest thing to such a flower is

Cosmos is in many parts of South Africa almost a symbol of Easter. This dramatic arrangement of these simple but striking flowers provides a warm welcome to guests over the holiday period.

Golden rod (*Solidago canadensis*) provided an excellent source of colour for this midsummer Golden Wedding party table.

This birthday arrangement involved little work and very few flowers. A central candle had been removed from a large candelabrum and replaced with a cup holder containing a bundle of chicken wire held in position by florist's tape. Using small garden chrysanthemums, cut short, a posy-like arrangement was made combining a variety of small flowers and maidenhair fern to soften the edges, finally dropping in a few snippets of plumbago. Then carrying on the colour theme of blue for a boy a few more sprigs of plumbago were used to decorate the birthday cake.

probably the HT rose 'Silver Star', a silvery-lilac coloured bloom with tinges of pink.

There was a time when no well-dressed man would have been seen in public without a buttonhole, but today these are generally reserved for special occasions, particularly weddings. There are a number of flowers extremely suitable for this purpose, such as gardenias, camellias, carnations and especially roses, but violets and even the primrose-like flowers of the *Primula veris* may be used. For people living in the Cape, the ericas and heathers provide wonderful buttonhole material.

Among the garden annuals there are many useful varieties, such as miniature zinnias, asters, seed dahlias and the small English daisies (*Bellis perennis*).

The rose is one of the most popular of all buttonhole flowers and the best for this purpose are nicely shaped, medium-sized varieties with tight buds, such as the glorious red 'Exciting' and the pale pink 'Sylvia'. Many of the miniatures are also excellent choices, among them being the blood-red 'Dwarf King', with its shapely buds, the small-budded 'Starina', a scarlet-vermilion rose with a creamy-white reverse, and 'Rosmarin' which has silvery blooms with scarlet centres.

It is important to include a little foliage with buttonholes and with roses it is a good idea to use their own leaves, but for many, such as carnations, you may use snippets of gypsophila, asparagus, nandina or other feathery greenery.

Although not a special occasion in the normal sense, there are often times when one needs flowers for someone in hospital and here it is important to consider easy to handle varieties, flowers that last well and particularly flowers that are not too large. Although the nurses love the flowers as much as the patients do, they are a lot of work and often cause a problem in public wards where space is limited. Small neat arrangements are appreciated.

Posy-like arrangements are more suitable for hospitals and for these chrysanthemums, particularly the small daisy-type, and carnations fit the bill admirably – both for their size and their long-lasting qualities.

Roses, particularly the miniatures, make delightful small arrangements, as do violets, whilst the bulb family provides many a fresh offering, especially daffodils. Sweet peas are easy and always popular and alstroemerias with their gay colours are excellent hospital flowers.

Always remember when sending flowers to hospitals, never to use red and white together. The combination may be stunning but unfortunately it is taboo. The medical fraternity, for some extraordinary reason, considers it unlucky, a notion so firmly held by doctors and nurses that they will not even accept such arrangements into a hospital.

ARRANGEMENT 1: For a lovely cool-looking display for our normally scorching Christmas days – use only white 'Iceberg' roses. Little work is involved and most of it may be done in advance.

You will need an oval entrée dish on short legs (a pyrex dish may be used as well), and a piece of oasis to fill the dish. The oasis should be covered in 5 cm gauge chicken wire and to keep it firm secure it to the rim of the bowl with either florist's wire or tape. Soak the oasis in water for an hour before using it.

The roses and greenery should be picked the night before, with stems no more than 12 cm to 15 cm long, and must be given a good deep drink of tepid water.

The actual arranging is simple. First a candle or two should be inserted in the centre of the oasis. Then your snippets of asparagus, ivy, fern or conifer should be interspersed all over the block to ensure the correct shape. After this it is merely a matter of filling the bowl with the clustered 'Iceberg' heads. Finally include a number of baubles or even ribbons to give it a Christmas look.

For the illustrated arrangement, blue and silver were used to emphasize coolness. When securing these ornaments, first remove the pins used for hanging the baubles, then stick into each hole a pipe cleaner bent double at the top to ensure a firm fit.

The advantage of this arrangement is that

A cool-looking table arrangement for a hot Christmas day – 'Iceberg' roses with blue candles and a few shiny baubles.

it is easily adaptable to suit your needs and the flowers you have available at the time. You don't have to use 'Icebergs', nor do you need to have a one flower grouping – you could just as well use mixed flowers.

If it is a small arrangement you want, use a round bowl with a single candle. For a long table use the large arrangement in the middle and a smaller bowl at either end.

Although the white 'Icebergs', blue candles and ornaments are most striking, there are many equally exciting combinations. As few gardens are without white daisy bushes, these could easily replace the roses, while the 'Ruby Red' or ordinary pink daisies would look very attractive with shocking pink baubles. A cheery arrangement could also be fashioned from yellow daisies, yellow candles and gold baubles.

Remember that daisies must have a very good drink of water before arranging. Their stems should be no longer than 10 cm to 12 cm. Daisies do not last well in oasis – it is best to use crumpled chicken wire. Always top up the water daily.

Another flower generally available in the garden during the Christmas season is the geranium and an arrangement of a bright red variety with either conifer leaves or combined with silver and green baubles, gives a festive look.

Most gardens will have some roses flowering around Christmas time and any of these may be used. I suggested 'Icebergs' only because they are the most prolifically blooming member of the rose family. They flower for so long that many people are reluctant to prune and so stop them flowering when July comes around. Do give them their well-deserved rest, they will bloom that much more abundantly the following season.

ARRANGEMENT 2: All that is needed for this arrangement is one red carnation – which could be substituted by a rose such as 'Exciting' or 'Satchmo' or any bright flower – a bright bauble, a bow and a specimen vase.

The carnation should be cut so that roughly two-thirds of the stem remains above the rim of the vase. To support this, use other lengths of stem cut to show the naturally curling leaves. A bauble attached to the stem by a piece of green florist's wire and a soft green bow complete the arrangement. This easy to prepare little charmer may be used either as a table or breakfast tray arrangement or even as a gift.

A single carnation to accompany a breakfast tray or a tray for someone spending Christmas in bed looks very cheery with its ribbon and bright bauble.

ARRANGEMENT 3: Though equally simple this decoration – a Christmas tree made of carnations – requires more flowers and more time.

You will need thirty carnations, three boxes of small baubles, small sprays of asparagus fern, snippets of pine needles and any other greenery you choose to use, such as tiny conifer cones, ivy or holly leaves, a container 25 cm high and 25 cm wide, a block of oasis wrapped in small-gauge wire netting, pipe-cleaners and thin florist's wire for binding the oasis to the container.

Your container should be stemmed, pref-

erably with ears to which the wire for binding the oasis may be fixed. Proceed as follows:

● Wrap oasis in wire mesh and leave in water to soak for several hours.

● With florist's clay firmly fix a small pin-holder in centre of container and press the oasis brick, on end, onto the pin-holder. Secure this to vase with florist's wire.

● With the shape of the Christmas tree in mind, start covering the block with greenery, graduating from narrow at top to wider at bottom.

● Once again bearing the shape of a tree in mind, place a carnation with a longer stem at the top – like the fairy at the top of the tra-ditional Christmas tree – then fill in evenly with the remaining 29 flowers. The car-nations should have been left up to their necks in water overnight. Before use cut the stems at sharp angles between the notches to make it easier to stick them into the oasis and for the flowers to drink more readily.

● To complete the arrangement, remove the springs from the baubles and replace with lengths of pipe cleaners, bent at the tip and pushed firmly into the baubles. Fill in with these between the flowers. The final ef-fect is utterly charming and very Christ-massy.

The red carnations were chosen for several reasons – red is a cheerful Yule-tide colour, carnations are easy to grow or to buy for those living in flats or with gardens too small for such luxuries. In addition, car-nations keep well as cut flowers, often last-ing for a whole week at a time.

To keep the decoration looking good, fill the bowl of the container with water im-mediately you complete the arrangement and always keep the top of the oasis block wet by topping with water at regular inter-vals.

Fragrant carnations have been popular for many centuries and have been developed over the years from rather puny small things into hybrids with large and very attractive flowers. They have long been popular not only because they are one of the best cut flowers available but also because they are easy to grow.

Two factors will ensure their successful cultivation – good drainage and free air movement. Although they will grow in practically any soil with the exception of very heavy clay, it is wise to add quantities of good well-rotted kraal manure or com-post and coarse sand several weeks before planting. Follow this up a few weeks later

with a fine sprinkling of lime over the whole area as carnations do not enjoy an acid soil.

Happiest in full sun positions, they are generally best grown in beds on their own. In fact, they are not very attractive bedding plants as they usually need staking; they are one of the flowers best grown in your private cutting garden well away from the public gaze; you may even grow them in straight commercial rows.

For really successful carnations it is necessary to disbud occasionally, for if left to grow on their own they will develop masses of rather inferior flowers. By picking off excess buds, you will produce lovely blooms on strong stems.

Thirty carnations, a few baubles and a little greenery make a delightful but simple to prepare Christmas tree for a lunch or dinner table.

ARRANGEMENT 4: Because hydrangeas are flowering at their best at Christmas time, they are a natural choice for festive decorations. One of the easiest possible arrangements is simply to use one large flower – they are often about 40 cm across – together with a few snippets of maidenhair fern.

The only props for this arrangement are a large but shallow cake plate, one head of an hydrangea – no treatment necessary – two green candles and a low, rather flat candle holder which can stand in water (or fasten the candles in position on plate with florist's clay). Finally have available a green tablecloth, three large green Christmas baubles plus a number of smaller ones in different shades of green.

Place the large flowerhead in the plate with the candlesticks to the back and side of it. Arrange the baubles about the flower before finally tucking in the sprigs of maiden-hair fern. The whole arrangement, once you have gathered together your material, will take no more than a few minutes to create. The only preparation of plant material necessary is to cut off the entire stem of the hydrangea in order that it may float, while the fern stems should be singed over a flame.

ARRANGEMENT 5: Succulents were used to great effect for another instant arrangement. Water is not necessary with this decoration as the succulents will last for over a week without any moisture.

You will need a flat bowl with a large pin-holder, two candles and any variety of succulent. Particularly suitable are the rose-shaped varieties. Baubles, tinsel or beads may be added.

First the pinholder should be fastened with florist's clay. Insert the candles into the pin-holder. Starting with the taller succu-lents at the back, work forward to the rose varieties. Finally drape the various decorations to suit your table.

Christmas with a truly South African feel to it is provided by this easy to prepare arrangement of succulents, baubles and beads backed by a simple arrangement of proteas in a beautiful copper jug.

A single hydrangea flower head, a few props, and pow – a simple but stunning festive table decoration!

XIII *Floral art — East and West*

Cutting flowers to brighten our home interiors is such a natural instinct that its origins are lost in the mists of time but even in the world's earliest pictures bunches of flowers are to be seen decorating altars. Excavations in caves in recent years have shown that there may even have been a Neanderthal Constance Spry.

Decorating the home or the altar with cut flowers is an ancient art, practised all over the world since earliest times. We know that the Egyptians and Greeks used lotus and acanthus leaves for decoration, and records show that flower arranging as a discipline began in Japan in about the sixth century AD, having been imported from China along with other Buddhist religious rituals.

For many years there were two main flower arranging disciplines: the Orient's gentle art of Ikebana – the arranging of living material – and the West's 'traditional' voluptuous mass arrangements, which are virtually a celebration of Mother Nature's colourful abundance. However, in recent years the West has developed a variety of styles. These include freestyle, naturalistic and even abstract, with one of the most popular today being the 'modern' approach, where expression is rather personal and interpretive, bound by few rules. Strangely all these styles owe more to Eastern than Western art.

The various techniques are all interesting but if you have no knowledge of them, don't let that stop you from doing your own thing. There is no reason why you should not enliven your home with simple arrangements. Don't take on the decoration of a church unless you know what you are doing, but do go ahead and use your instincts with colour, texture, balance, scale and harmony and you will produce decorations that will not only delight yourself but your family and friends as well.

Knowledge in flower arranging, as in all things, increases your pleasure and once you get started you will want to learn more. This is easily done, by way of any of the many hundreds of flower arranging books on the market or, if you have the time, by joining a flower club or Ikebana school. For a start it would be useful to know a little about the two main streams, the linear style of the East based on a focal point, and the massed arrangements of the West. Later you will probably channel your talent and interest into one or other of these fields.

While the Western style grew naturally out of a desire to make the most of the quantities of flowers and foliage available, the Ikebana method has its origins in religious and philosophical symbolism. From this developed an art which today displays the Japanese appreciation of simplicity and economy of line – values evident both in their art and the stark interior decor of their homes. Orientals would rather contemplate the perfection of one exquisite chrysanthemum than the overpowering splendour of a dozen opulent peonies.

Economics also play a part in the various styles of arranging. In the West large

The two main streams of floral art are the Western style or the massed arrangement, and the Eastern Ikebana style which is linear and based on a focal point.

135

gardens have been popular over the centuries and are still much in evidence in South Africa today, so obtaining quantities of foliage and flowers for massed arrangements has never been a problem. Today, however, this is no longer so in Europe or even in South Africa. Not surprisingly the great expansion of the duplex and simplex townhouse styles of living is having an effect on gardening in general. Flower arranging is of necessity becoming simpler as the smaller gardens produce fewer flowers, although we have not yet reached the stage of Japan, where home gardens, if any at all, are so small that practically all floral material has to be bought.

Of course flower arrangements also have to suit their setting. A simple magnolia with a little foliage would look ridiculous in an overstuffed Victorian drawing room with busy wall-paper and heavy drapes. Cottagey homes, too, although requiring natural styles, do need rather fuller arrangements.

The word 'mass' makes the massed Western-style arrangement sound rather heavy when in fact this is not the case. Although a lot of material may be used, the aim generally is for lightness, and in modern arrangements the trend is towards even fewer flowers. Exponents of this style often seek to portray the dramatic, with bold leaves and exotic forms. They prefer strong colours and unusual containers, often accompanied by ornaments or accessories such as stones, driftwood, seed-pods and shells.

Although in Victorian times the circular arrangement was favoured, the classical triangular shape took over and reigned supreme – with strong lines being popular for many years. Fashions change, however, and in recent times there has once again been a swing away from the often harsh linear forms of the post-war era to a softer, more flowing style. Many of today's Western designers seem to be seeking a touch of romance rather than practicality.

Ikebana designs are of course ideal for use in the uncluttered Japanese surroundings and also in many modern Western homes – and this is why at exhibitions they are always best set off against stark white rice paper screens.

These simple yet impressive arrangements are expressions of spring by two different Ikebana artists.

A number of Ikebana schools of various disciplines have taken root in South Africa in recent years. This art form is becoming increasingly popular but it is interesting to note that in Japan there are in fact many hundreds of Ikebana disciplines, although the 'big three' are Ikenobo (the oldest and founder of Ikebana as we know it), Sogetsu (modern) and Ohara.

IKENOBO

This school was founded more than 500 years ago and arrangements range from elegantly simple – the very classical Shoka which requires very little material to the rather complex but spectacular 2 m to 5 m tall Rikka arrangements. The modern Ikenobo school arrangements are very pleasing, reflecting the arranger's skill in the most subtle manner.

SOGETSU

The most modern of the schools. It is possible with this discipline to create very avant-garde arrangements – but it is necessary to study the basic styles thoroughly in order to develop a sense of proportion, space, colour and depth before going on to unusual designs and materials.

OHARA

Of the 'big three' this school is the closest to nature. By following a syllabus of lessons, one can progress from beautiful line arrangements to landscapes and finally to the simple Bunjin style, based on the Chinese Literati paintings, and to the more decorative Rimpa style, based on the paintings of the Edo era.

In South Africa the most widely practised disciplines are two modern schools, Sogetsu and Ichiyo, and the more traditional Ohara.

An important reason for the great interest in Ikebana is that it teaches more than just flower arranging; it also encourages pupils to appreciate nature and to make the most of all the plants and objects in the garden. Exponents of this art quite rightly believe that, if you look around you will find even in the dullest garden, in the dreariest season, items which may be combined to make fascinating displays. Dry leaves and roots suddenly become things of beauty when arranged with care.

I was privileged to meet the great lady of

Even torn leaves are used to set the scene in this charming Ikebana water landscape, which breathes all the beauty of autumn.

137

the Ohara School of Ikebana – Italy's Mrs Jenny Banti-Pereira – when she visited South Africa a few years ago, and was amazed by her use of extraordinary material in arrangements. During one of her demonstrations the school's only Western Grand Master produced some sensational arrangements using such items as the half-rotted root of an old cycad, a dried Dutchman's pipe and even the lichen-covered branches of a tree.

None was more spectacular, however, than her example of a water garden. Preparing her water landscape, known in Japanese as *Mizumono*, she explained that it was necessary to try to capture in the vase the feeling, essence or atmosphere of what was actually seen in the living landscape. She impressed on her audience the importance of studying how things grow and using them as they would appear in nature – not in unnatural ways.

Using a flat bowl, *Suiban*, to represent a pond she included in her arrangement some lotus leaves, Louisiana irises – roots and all – *Pontedaria cordata*, Rabbit foot ferns and water lily buds.

In Ikebana, landscape arrangements are always seasonal and the one produced by Mrs Banti-Pereira was autumnal, so it was not surprising that among the materials used were not only turning leaves but even some that were torn and tattered in order to give the arrangement a natural appearance.

It is also important to adherents of this school to use in the water only material which grows in water. As a result the fern, which in nature would grow at the side of the pond, is used in a similar position in the arrangement, indicating the point where water and earth meet.

Although a pinholder, *Kenzan*, is used to hold the material in place, it is given a natural look concealed beneath Louisiana iris roots.

The intention of this Japanese discipline is not a mere striving after beauty, but the creation of a scene or the expression in a vase of your impressions, moods and dreams. What is important is the act of arranging, the communion with nature and the search for simplicity and harmony.

Beauty is to be found everywhere in the garden by the Ikebana enthusiast who sees loveliness in stark lichen-covered branches (top) and the roots of an old cycad (centre).

Known as a one-row arrangement, some unlikely-looking material – to an untrained eye – is combined to make a beautiful Ikebana arrangement. Items used included reddish watsonia stems with dried seeds, plus watsonia flowers and a few sprays of our indigenous Wild dagga plant.

138

Ikebana is an art which requires years of study – it can become the work of a lifetime – and for the fullest appreciation of it, you need to know and understand plants, their form and their habits. In this the South African devotee has a tremendous advantage, even over the Japanese, for we in the Republic have both a greater variety of flora than anywhere in the world and the luxury of space and the opportunity to garden – often on a grand scale unknown in many countries in the world.

For anyone with the space, gardening for the Ikebana vase should be an exciting exercise. In addition to growing material for all seasons, the inclusion of a water garden can provide a new realm of interest by supplying a variety of material for use throughout the year.

Growing water plants is a fascinating pastime but they are often hard to come by in South Africa. Usually the best way of obtaining material is through friends or other water garden enthusiasts.

The easiest plants to find for a pond are water lilies. Fortunately these are among the most beautiful of all aquatic varieties and a must for any pond with sufficient depth. There are two important factors for the successful cultivation of these plants. First, they must be planted to allow for a stem of 30 cm from pond bottom to water surface or they will not grow, and secondly, they must be grown in full sunlight or the flowers will not open.

Also important when designing a pond is to ensure you know your city's by-laws, for in many cases if the pond has a depth of more than 30 cm you will need to fence off the area completely for the safety of children. In this case, when building your water feature, it is necessary to sink special holes to accommodate the roots of these exotic plants.

For good growth, water lilies need a rich soil and a mixture of one-third well-rotted manure to two-thirds garden soil. It is important to use old manure, as fresh manure encourages algal growth. Once planted the soil should be covered with a few centimetres of coarse river sand to prevent it from rising or being disturbed by the fish.

Do not overlook the inclusion of fish in your pond for they eat mosquito larvae and without them you could have a problem on your hands.

Other useful pond plants which are fairly easy to obtain are the Louisiana iris and *Pontederia cordata*. The pontederia, with its blue flowers and spear-shaped leaves is a most attractive and useful stand-by for arrangers. It must be grown in fairly shallow water. The Louisiana iris may be grown either at the

side of the pool or in containers in the pond. It enjoys having its roots wet but the plant itself should be above water level. For good flowering, additional phosphate should be added to the soil in the form of bone-meal or phosphate.

You need a really large pond to grow the lotus, for when established the leaves of this bold beauty may grow to more than a metre tall. They are a joy to behold, producing not only striking foliage but also handsome globular flowers.

There are a number of useful plants for around the edge of the pool such as the Japanese *Iris kaempferi*, which enjoys being near water, and the easy to grow indigenous irises – dietes (white) and moraea (yellow). Another useful indigenous plant is the spectacular *Lobelia cardinalis*. This 60 cm-tall plant has gorgeous beetroot-coloured leaves and brilliant scarlet flowers.

For the good health of the pond it is important to grow oxygenating plants but they are not always easily obtainable. Try to find *Vallisneria*, which has long narrow, rather ribbon-like leaves and *Myriophyllum*, commonly known as cat's tail waterplant and not to be confused with *Asparagus meyerii*.

Giving the impression of the extraordinary material and growth in South Africa, this dramatic arrangement was prepared by Mrs Jenny Banti-Pereira, the only Western Master of the Ohara Ikebana school. Ideal as a foyer decoration, it includes huge pieces of wood, a large ceramic bowl, leaves and flowers of a giant strelitzia, dry stems of a petrea bush and ginger with its shell-like flowers. Orchids (below) are combined with the stem of a palm seed head.

Useful plants for pond plantings:

WATER PLANTS

Cape water uintjie (*Aponogeton distachyos*) – white flowers, floating leaves

Cat's tail (*Myriophyllum*) – oxygenating

Papyrus grass (*P. antiquorum*) – will grow in water at the pond edge

Vallisneria – oxygenating

Water lettuce (*Pistia stratiotes*) – floating water cleanser

Water lilies (*Nymphaea* varieties) – attractive flowers

Water poppy (*Hydrocleys commersonni*) – attractive yellow flowers

BOG PLANTS

Arrow arum (*Peltrandra*) – flowers, foliage

Arum lily varieties (*Zantedeschia aethiopica*) – bold leaves, white and green blooms

Iris kaempferi – attractive flowers, foliage

Iris laevigata – flowers, foliage

Iris pseudacorus – flowers, foliage

Lobelia cardinalis – attractive purple foliage, scarlet flowers

Lobelia syphilitica – blue flowers

Louisiana iris – attractive flowers, foliage

Papyrus (*Cyperus papyrus*) – striking foliage

Pontederia cordata – distinctive spear-like foliage, blue flowers

Prickly rhubarb (*Gunnera manicata*) – enormous leaves

Umbrella bush (*Cyperus alternifolius*)

POND-SIDE PLANTS

Ajuga reptans varieties – ground covers with interesting leaf colours, blue flowers

Astilbe – lovely plume-like blooms, feathery foliage

Creeping Jenny (*Lysimachia nummularia* 'Aurea') – groundcover with attractive yellow-green leaf

Day lily (*Hemerocallis* varieties) – lovely flowers in many colours

Fern varieties – attractive foliage

Hosta – foliage

Meadow rue (*Thalictrum flavum*) – delicate foliage, fluffy flowers

Pampas grass (*Cortaderia selloana*) – tall plant with plumes

Saxifrage (*Bergenia*) – attractive round leaves, pink flowers

Among the plants suitable for poolside growth few can be as prolific and attractive as the fast-spreading and striking arum lily. Only one is needed to liven a simple Ikebana arrangement (right).

The stately Louisiana iris, although delicate in appearance, is an easy to grow bog plant, which not only looks delightful at the side of the pool but may be grown in tubs in the water. They also make excellent cut flowers.

XIV Good enough to eat

Flowers may be used to decorate anything but one of their most charming uses is with food – adding a touch of style to the ordinary. Eye appeal plays an important role in the presentation of food and the garden can provide a whole range of charming trims for dishes.

Restaurateurs appreciate the fact that 'people eat with their eyes' and you will always note in the reviews of dining critics that presentation is one of the important considerations.

But whether in a restaurant or a home it is always the host or hostess who puts that little bit of extra effort into presenting dishes attractively who earns the plaudits.

Nor do the decorations have to be extravagant – often they are all the more charming for their simplicity. Your guests will remember the rose or hibiscus on their napkin or the simple table decoration you have prepared because it shows that you care and that you have been eager to please them.

You can't disguise bad food with decoration but you can make good food look special by taking a little extra trouble with your presentation. To show you how easy it is to add a little glamour to your dishes – using drinks and salads, cheeseboards and desserts as 'vases' – I have included recipes and photographs of some presentations that have impressed my wife and me at restaurants and hotels around the world, often simple trimmings costing nothing more than the few minutes taken to pick the flowers. A fine ripe brie is an excellent cheese for rounding off a meal but it can look dull dumped on the board beside a knife; add only the head of one beautiful geranium and it looks fit for a feast.

A well-known Durban hotel offers diners in its rooftop restaurant a dessert of Italian Kisses – those delightful little chocolate-coated ice-creams that are available at supermarkets. Normally they would look like any other bowl of chocolates but instead they are presented on crushed ice in small glass elephants, with a flower saucily angled like a hat on the forehead. The effect is marvellous! Practically any flower may be used but carnations look particularly good.

Drinks too may be given a boost with the addition of a few sprigs of mint or flowers. An hibiscus bloom floating in the punch elevates it from the commonplace to the exotic. And for an attractive buffet display, foliage can add an exciting touch – either ivy for decoration or the large leaves of the ornamental banana (*Musa ensete*) and the giant strelitzia (*S. nicolai*) as 'containers', piled high with luscious fruits and interspersed once again with hibiscus flowers.

In English pubs Pimms cups are made to look irresistible to pre-lunch drinkers by garnishing the frosted silver mugs and glasses with slices of apple and orange, a maraschino cherry and a sprig of mint, plus borage flowers and leaves. These sky-blue flowers look beautiful and give a cucumber flavour to the drink.

Agapanthus, those spectacular indigen-

PINECONE CHEESE SPREAD

250 g whole almonds
500 g cream cheese
½ cup mayonnaise
5 crisply cooked bacon slices, crumbled
1 tablespoon chopped green onion
½ teaspoon dill weed
⅛ teaspoon pepper
Agapanthus umbels for decoration

Spread a single layer of almonds in a shallow pan. Bake at 150°C for 15 minutes, until the almonds begin to turn colour.

Combine the softened cream cheese and mayonnaise. Add the bacon, onion, dill and pepper and mix well. Cover and chill overnight. Form the cheese mixture into the shape of two pinecones on a board or serving platter. Beginning at the narrow end, press the almonds at an angle into the cheese mixture to form rows. Continue overlapping the rows until all the cheese is covered. Garnish with sprigs of cut agapanthus umbels. Serve with biscuits.

Agapanthus umbels (left), stripped of their seed heads and cut to shape look remarkably like pine needles and are used for this purpose (right) to decorate the pine cone made of cheese, when no pine trees were available.

Cheese boards can look ordinary if presented with only cheese and a knife – the addition of a few flowers make the presentation much more attractive.

Simple Italian Kisses served with coffee after a meal take on a new dimension when served on crushed ice in attractive little elephant shaped glass dishes with a fresh flower placed saucily over the forehead.

ous flowers that seem to grow well in most gardens, are not only striking when in bloom but their umbels are also useful after the flowers fade. With seedheads removed they are suitable for various arrangements, looking rather like pine needles. A clever use of these was seen in America where a restaurant presented a cheese spread in the form of pine cones, made with almonds and umbels for foliage.

'Please don't eat the daisies,' goes an old Doris Day song – but do try the nasturtiums, they're delicious. Not only do they add a touch of colour to a salad but also con-

Nasturtium flowers are not only attractive, they are good enough to eat. They add a peppery flavour to a green salad.

tribute a delightful peppery taste, combining particularly well with chervil to make an excellent dish. Also lending more than just colour, the petals of calendulas (*C. officinalis*) when sprinkled on the top of soup act as a thickening agent.

An extremely useful plant to have in your garden is the elderberry tree (*Sambucus nigra*) or the golden elder (*S. racemosa* 'Plumosa Aurea'), for in addition to many fine qualities its lacy white flowers are as edible as they are attractive. South Africa's herb expert, Margaret Roberts, serves in her home wonderful fritters made with whole elderberry flowers which not only look delightful but are delicious. They may also be used in a variety of cakes and puddings.

While on the subject of eating flowers try

NASTURTIUM AND SPROUT SALAD
1 small lettuce
1 cup (100 g) nasturtium flowers
1 cup Mung bean sprouts
3 tablespoons olive oil
1 ½ tablespoons lemon juice
salt and pepper
1 tablespoon chopped chervil
Wash and drain well your fresh sprouts, nasturtium flowers and lettuce – preferably the soft variety. Dry ingredients on kitchen paper towels, taking care not to bruise the flowers. Just before serving, blend the salad dressing by shaking well together the oil, lemon juice and seasoning in a screw-topped bottle. Pour over the flowers and sprinkle the dish with the chopped chervil. Serves 4.

serving a delectable Italian dish – flowers of pumpkin or marrow stuffed with savoury mince meat. And, what is more you won't ruin your future vegetable crop, for I am told you use only the male flowers.

Many blooms may be crystallized to make lovely decorations for cakes and desserts such as trifle. Excellent for this purpose are rose petals and violet flowers, plus the stems of angelica – that popular arranger's herb – which when cut provides green leaf motifs.

Requiring a little more effort than some of the other presentations but making a stunning final luncheon course is a simple ice-cream served in a floral ice mould which keeps the dessert from melting.

Seen at a terrace buffet in Nice, the ice ring was made using a ring cake mould filled with roses and 'cast' in ice. The trick, we discovered from the chef, was to use crushed ice. Put a layer of powdered ice at the bottom of the ring and on top of this place a number of roses or other flowers facing downwards onto the ice. Fill in around the flowers with more powdered ice. When the whole mould is filled with the crushed ice place in the deep-freeze until set. Finally when frozen remove and pour iced water over it to fill in any gaps or crevices. Return to the deep-freeze to set. It takes a little time but it's easy and the result splendid.

A floral ice mould – which gives glimpses of roses and foliage – makes an excellent container for keeping icecream chilled for a party.

PARTY PUNCH

1 medium-size pineapple
250 g castor sugar or icing sugar
6 bottles dry white wine
1 litre bottle soda water
1 litre bottle lemonade
1 bottle medium dry champagne
Two or three hibiscus flowers for decoration

Peel the pineapple and cut into cubes, add sugar and one bottle of wine. (If you use canned pineapple don't add sugar). Pour into an earthenware container and refrigerate overnight.

Chill the remaining wine, soda, lemonade, and champagne until very cold. Mix at the last moment adding champagne last. Finally pour into a punch bowl over a large block of ice. A nice touch is to freeze flowers or fruit into the ice block, with just a few drops of green colouring added to the water to make the ice glow. Float your hibiscus on top of the punch.

An English pub-style Pimm's Cup appears more appealing on a hot summer's day when decorated with slices of apple, orange and maraschino cherries, plus a sprig of mint and another of that charming herb borage, which adds colour with its sky blue flowers and introduces a cucumber flavour to the drink.

XV   Treated treasure

Economy with plant material is one of the most important attributes of any flower arranger. Few gardens contain so much material that anyone can afford to squander their treasures. The aim should be to try to keep vases looking fresh and lovely for as long as possible. This not only saves a tremendous amount of time in preparing arrangements but also leaves sufficient blooms in the garden to keep it looking pretty at the same time.

Keeping your cut material in good condition starts long before you actually begin work on your design, even before you cut your first flower – for a lot depends on the way in which you grow your plants. Well-fed, watered and pruned plants will not only produce bigger, better and more beautiful blooms but also stronger plants which, if cared for when cut, will do far better than would puny, unloved and poorly tended material.

There are many items to consider when preparing your arrangement. These include when to cut your material, how to cut it, how to carry it, maintaining it in good condition until you actually start arranging, treating it to make it last as long as possible, the condition of the vase and the water you put into it, and finally how to maintain the arrangement in the vase for the longest possible time once the design is complete.

This sounds an awful lot of work, but it is nothing of the sort, merely a matter of routine. Most of the things you do become second nature, so that you never even think about them, much of the work being merely comonsense and automatic.

PLAN FOR ARRANGING

The following is a routine which will help you in preparing an arrangement, from the picking stage to the final topping up of vases with water.

WHEN TO CUT

For busy people, picking time must often be when they have spare moments available but fortunately the best times to cut flowers are at the end of the day – late afternoon or early evening, when most people have completed their daily labours – or first thing in

Proteas dry well while in fresh arrangements but should later be hung up individually in a dark, dry place until needed again.

the morning, before you really start your programme for the day.

Many people find that picking late in the day is the most practical and successful time, for it not only allows time to prepare your material – by singeing, boiling, bruising ends or whatever – but it leaves the whole night in which to soak your flowers and foliage, enabling them to absorb water, to fill their stems and become crisp and turgid.

Fresh or dried delicate pink Blushing bride proteas make for sensational arrangements. They dry very easily but after use in a fresh arrangement are best hung upside down so that their heads are facing upwards when later re-used in the vase.

MATERIAL CHOICE

Choose blooms to be cut very carefully.

- Blooms should be unblemished.
- Most are best picked before full bloom, with buds just showing colour. However, pick blossom when in tight bud; it will open in the warmth of the home.
- The only open blooms you should cut are those for use as focal points and which can easily be replaced as they fade.
- It is wise to pick flowers such as peonies, roses, irises and poppies before buds open; flowers with spires, such as gladiolus, are best cut when some buds are just opening and others are giving glimpses of colour.

HOW TO CUT

It is vital to use sharp clean tools, either a knife or secateurs. A knife is preferable for a sharp blade makes a good clean cut, while cutters are inclined to squeeze stems. As it is at the point of cutting that stems absorb water it is important that they have as large an area for absorption as possible. The best way to ensure this is to cut stems at an angle. There are several other advantages in this:

- a stem cut at a slant cannot rest flat on the base of the vase or pin-holder, cutting off the supply of water
- more cells are exposed for intake of water
- stems at a slant are easier to split.

Many plants may be cut at any point along the stem, but for those with sectioned hollow stems it is advisable to cut through a link node.

PRUNING

When picking use the opportunity to prune as you go. Roses, for instance, should be cut just above a plump node, preferably one facing outwards, as this will force out another flowering spike at this point, ensuring healthy and floriferous plants.

While cutting consider the shape of your plant and prune in such a way as to maintain a good form while also inducing more growth. Long stems should be cut from rose

bushes, ensuring that the bush remains low and well branched, rather than tall and leggy.

Once established you will do little harm in taking pickings from such fast growing plants as the abelias and cotoneasters, but be very careful with the azaleas and gardenias – these should not be heavily picked. Take care that in cutting you do not ruin their shape, it is not every plant that takes kindly to too much pruning.

When picking it is important to plunge the stems into tepid water immediately and it is worth carrying a bucket around with you as you work. It is also best, where possible, to keep the cut flowers in the shade while you are working – particularly if you are placing your flowers in a basket rather than a bucket. The longer stems are kept out of water the more time they have to absorb air. Pleasurable though it be, picking should take as little time as possible so that you can get your flowers into the house and start treating them.

If for some reason flowers have been kept out of water for a little while, cut the stems at an angle underwater before giving them a long drink of water. While some flowers such as proteas may be kept out of water for long periods without any treatment whatever, sometimes lasting a few days without any water, the majority are not so blessed and certainly if you are travelling any distance it would be wise to wrap the stems of your flowers in damp cotton wool and thick damp newspaper covered with tinfoil.

HANDLING CUT MATERIAL

Your first move is to clean up your pickings, removing thorns, unnecessary foliage and excess buds around the flowers.

The next step is to ensure that stems are able to absorb as much water as possible. There are several methods of doing this:

- hard woody stems (such as those of prunus, flowering quince or hawthorns) should be either split or crushed. It is also important to scrape away some of the bark at the end of stems.
- Flowers with hollow stems, such as dahlias, poppies, delphiniums and larkspurs should have about 5–10 cm of stem dipped in boiling water for about three minutes. Always be careful to protect flower heads during this process. With some of the thicker hollow-stemmed plants, such as snow on the mountain (*Euphorbia marginata*), it is even possible

Poppies picked in bud open in the vase.

The bright terracotta red of the Chinese hat plant (Holmskioldia) is extremely useful in winter gardens. Flowering from late summer until well into winter it provides splashes of bright colour to otherwise dull surroundings and if mature stems are chosen lasts well in the vase.

Autumn foliage looks beautiful on the plant and may be used for autumn arrangements but alas, the leaves fall too rapidly once cut. Dipping stems in melted beeswax can, however, delay this process.

to fill stems with water with a syringe and then stop them up to retain moisture longer. Water lilies also benefit from having the tips of their stems plunged into boiling water briefly before being filled with a syringe. Another trick which competition enthusiasts use to preserve water lilies is to drop lukewarm paraffin into the centre of the flowers to prevent them from closing.

- By using a candle flame or that of a spirit burner, plants with stems exuding a milky substance, such as frangipani or poinsettia, can be singed to seal the ends of their stems.

Once treated in one of the ways suggested above, your flowers should be placed in deep lukewarm water and kept overnight in a cool place, ready for arranging in the morning.

Some flowers, such as hydrangeas, arums and cannas, benefit from being totally immersed in water. Violets undoubtedly last better if floated in tepid water for a few hours before use.

With the exception of the grey-leafed varieties with felty surfaces, most foliage absorbs moisture through leaves and stems and thus it is best to immerse the entire length of your greenery in water. The beautiful large, veined caladium leaves, which range in colour from a silver white to blush, rose and dark red, will last for up to two weeks in the vase if their ends are split and they are left upright in water overnight.

Ferns benefit greatly from being left immersed in water overnight. The dainty and delicate maidenhair fern lasts extremely well in the vase, in bouquets and in corsages if the ends of the stems are burned. This is essential no matter how short the stems may be, and if you find you need to cut them again, they must again be briefly singed with a candle before use.

Autumn foliage makes for beautiful arrangements but sadly it does not always last very long before leaves start to fall, but it helps if you dip the ends of stems in melted beeswax.

With flowers which have to be twisted or tugged rather than cut from a plant, such as arum lilies, it is necessary to cut away all the soft white part at the end of the stems before allowing them to soak. Other flowers that should have the white tips removed from their stems before soaking are daffodils, violets, hyacinths, irises and tulips, because they only drink from the green part of their stems.

It is also necessary with plants such as agapanthus and members of the narcissus family which exude a sticky substance when cut, to wash this away under a running tap, or it tends to block their stems.

Some plants have stems which demonstrate a certain wilfulness in changing shape once arranged. One such plant is the tulip which is inclined to flop unless you keep the stems tightly wrapped in damp newspaper for several hours, preferably overnight, to help stiffen them.

Remember, with your actual arrangement, that flowers last much longer in clean vases and the best way of ensuring this is to wash all your containers in bleach. Alternately, when washed in the dish-washer they will come out sparkling and sterilized. *All* equipment should be kept clean and items such as wire netting and pinholders should be rinsed in disinfectant after use.

Adding to your vase water some commercial life-extender or a capful of bleach to reduce algal growth ensures that material will last much longer; it is necessary when changing water to replace the chemicals. Products such as these reduce the possibility of wilting and retard the opening of buds. Another simple way of keeping water clean and fresh is to drop a piece of charcoal into the bottom of your vase.

Although arrangers generally have their own thoughts about life-extenders for their flowers, with methods ranging from mineral waters to aspirin or sugar, it has been shown that commercial products for this

Short pieces of *bougainvillea* 'Natalia' oven dried and wired together were used for this small arrangement for a guest bedroom.

152

purpose are really much more effective, while sugar in some cases actually clogs stems by encouraging bacterial growth.

Throughout the life of the arrangement it will be necessary to keep topping up your container with water and you will often be surprised how much water is consumed, especially straight after arranging. It also benefits the flowers to be misted occasionally with water, because some plants, such as hydrangeas, absorb moisture through their flower heads.

Should you use green floral foam for an arrangement, always ensure that the brand name is facing upwards when you soak it, for the blocks are so designed that the capillary action works better in that direction and will absorb water far more quickly.

POSITIONING AN ARRANGEMENT

The placing of an arrangement in a room is also important in maintaining its condition. Its biggest enemy in the house is the draught, which causes the material to lose its moisture rapidly. It is also important never to place a vase in direct sunlight, under hot light bulbs or near powerful electric fans and heaters – especially fan-heaters. In air-conditioned rooms it is advisable to mist arrangements occasionally with a little water.

SPECIAL TREATMENTS

Arrangers, particularly those who grow their own flowers and foliage, soon get to know their material, and become expert at keeping it fresh for as long as possible, but there are some plants which benefit from special treatment. These include:

BAMBOO VARIETIES

Cuttings of this charming plant may be induced to last for several months after being cut:
• cut a number of bamboo stems, removing the top of each stem by cutting just below a node so that you can fill the hollow section remaining with water
• drill small holes on either side of each section lower down the stem, so that these too may be filled with water
• ensure when cutting through a node that it is level in order to stand more easily
• once each section is filled with water you will find that shoots sprout from the sides, providing magnificent foliage material which you may use in arrangements over many months.

BOUGAINVILLEA

Cut only when mature, remove all leaves,

Statice varieties, like the everlastings, dry naturally, retaining their colour very well.

split the ends and submerge stems and flowers in a bath of water until all florets are crisp and papery in texture. A method suitable for small pieces of bougainvillea is to put about 5 cm of stem in boiling water containing a tablespoonful of vinegar and leave for about an hour, then hang up immediately to dry.

CAMELLIA

Never cut long stems of *C. japonica* or you will spoil not only the bush but the following season's buds too. Blossoms should be only partly open when cut and stems should immediately be placed in damp cotton wool. Spray with a fine mist and place in the fridge for a short while. Later split stem ends and keep in cold water overnight. Try never to handle camellia blooms as they bruise very easily.

DAHLIAS

All varieties benefit from having ends dipped in boiling water after cutting and then placed in a weak solution of potassium nitrate.

HYDRANGEAS

It is better to break the stem than to cut it. Scrape away bark and place in boiling water for a few moments.

MARIGOLD VARIETIES (Tagetes)

It is most important to put marigolds into water immediately after cutting as water loss early on stops maturation. You should not pick marigolds until they are about three-quarters open as buds do not open very successfully after cutting.

PUSSYWILLOW (Salix discolor)

May be forced indoors when buds are just over a quarter mature. If stem ends are split 153 and placed in cold water, the catkins will open in the warmth of the house.

PRESERVING

Flowers and arrangements, sadly, cannot last forever, but flower arrangers have discovered ways of capturing their ephemeral beauty by preserving them beyond their naturally allotted life-span.

The methods of preserving flowers are various and include hanging up to dry, desiccating with special chemicals, pressing and preserving with glycerine. When flowers are few, particularly in winter, or when you are in a hurry and have no time to collect a lot of foliage, it is extremely useful to be able to turn to preserved material. Beautiful arrangements are produced using dried flowers, grasses, foliage, seed pods, the branches of trees, old roots and driftwood, even charred bits of wood from the bushveld. They can be used not only in dried arrangements but also as fillers with fresh flowers.

Attractive as dried arrangements are, it is still necessary to keep on livening them up, changing their position and re-arranging them. There is nothing as dreary as a dusty dry arrangement which has been left in one position for too long. 'Dries' need tidying up now and then, damaged pieces removed and new material included.

Except for the most delicate pieces it does your dry material very little harm to be taken out onto the lawn every now and then and to be hosed down with the fine mist spray, as long as you once again allow the material to dry thoroughly before re-use. You may even rinse some of the tougher material under a tap.

The various methods of preserving are:

DRYING

Always pick unblemished material before it reaches its peak, then treat the ends of stems as you would for arranging fresh flowers – crushing, slitting or boiling – before giving a good long drink of water. Drying flowers should never be fully open or petals will fluff and fall.

Once the stems of flowers or foliage are turgid, hang up to dry. Grasses, bulrushes and the like may be hung in bunches but for delicate material it may be best to hang each stem individually. Most flower arrangers find wire hangers ideal for this purpose.

Material should be dried in a cellar, unused garage, warm attic or in a dark basement. Darkness is important, for if dried in the light, material becomes brittle. Ensure that there is good air circulation and that the

Dried flowers may be used in many ways from mini-arrangements to formal vases and look particularly good in basketware.

When fresh flowers are hard to come by dried arrangements are extremely useful, even spectacular, as this one shows, but don't allow them to become dusty and boring. Every now and again take yours outside and hose it down, remove any damaged pieces and rearrange with some new material, to keep it interesting and attractive.

Britain's internationally famous floral designer George Smith used seed heads, grasses and flowers for this striking and unusual dry arrangement prepared for a show during one of his regular demonstration visits to South Africa.

room is dry, for if there is any trace of damp your hangings will go mouldy.

It is most important with certain flowers to ensure that you pick mature material, particularly plants which form long bracts of flowers such as the glorious brick-coloured Chinese hatplant (Holmskioldia) and bougainvillea, where some blooms open before others. The moment to pick these is immediately the last florets open and mature. With both these plants it is also necessary to remove all the little leaves that grow between the florets.

Sulphur fumes may be used to retain the colour of dry bougainvillea:
• Lay bracts in long flat boxes lined with tin foil then place around them burning coals in shoe polish or other suitable flat tins
• Sprinkle Flowers of Sulphur over the burning coals and then seal boxes as quickly as possible to retain fumes.
• Leave box for several days before opening.

Two extremely useful long-stemmed plants are the thistle (Echinops ritro) and wild rhubarb (Acanthus mollis) with its tall flower spikes which dry very well if picked when the flowers are still looking fresh.

It is a good idea to allow flowers such as hydrangeas to dry in the vase. Keep the vase filled with water at first but then slowly reduce the water until the flowers are finally dry, whereupon you may either leave them in the vase or hang them up for use later. You may 'hang dry' almost anything but among the most useful material are the everlastings, such as Helipterum and Helichrysum, gypsophila, statice, grasses, reeds and bulrushes and some of the herbs, such as yarrow. Members of the protea family also dry extremely well and one of the most successful varieties is that dainty charmer, the Blushing bride (Serruria florida), which lasts very well fresh in a vase and may then be hung up to keep its flowers facing upwards. It will dry out totally and be ready for use in about a week.

To retain the colour of flowers, a light misting of varnish helps.

DESICCANTS

There are many of these used by keen arrangers, from simple dry sand, to borax, silica gel and even mealie meal. This method is particularly useful for large blooms such as peonies, roses, camellias, clematis and daffodils.

The method employed is to fill the bottom of a box with about 3 cm of desiccant. Gently lay your bloom on the surface and slowly filter the powder or crystals around the flower until it is totally covered. The

155

length of time needed to dry by this method varies greatly depending on the material and the desiccant chosen. Silica gel may dry your flowers in as little as three days while sand may take as long as 14 days.

It will not matter if you should forget your stems in the sand but take care with the gel as it can cause brittleness.

Although more expensive than the other methods the silica gel is by far the most efficient method, providing you do not allow your material to dry out too much.

PRESSING

Items suitable for pressing which may be included in arrangements are the large leaves, such as those of the aspidistra, and especially fern leaves. These all press very well between layers of newspaper under heavy telephone directories or other books. They are fit for use within about 10 weeks in humid areas but may be ready in as little as three to five weeks in dry inland areas.

GLYCERINE METHOD

Plants with shiny, dark-green leathery leaves, such as the aspidistra, loquat, laurel, magnolia, citrus, gardenia, privet and viburnum are particularly suitable for this method of preserving. Also very good are penny gum (florist's gum) and other eucalyptus varieties, plus pittosporum, cotoneaster, mahonia and ferns.

The method is to crush woody stem ends or split them and scrape away some of the bark in the normal way and then to plunge them into a bucket containing a mixture of one part glycerine to two parts of boiling water. This solution is absorbed quite rapidly and leaves tend to turn beautiful bronze-brown colours which are extremely effective in arangements. The leaves are ready for use when they acquire the colouring which suits your taste. You will find that while an aspidistra may take as long as eight weeks before it is ready, most of the plants – such as bay leaves, mahonia, magnolia, pittosporum and many others – take only three or four weeks.

Other plants suitable for preservation by this method include the lovely green Bells of Ireland, berberis, nandina, camellia and elaeagnus. Hydrangea heads dried by the glycerine method take on a beautiful creamy colour.

There are also plants which, while not drawing the glycerine up through their stems very effectively, may be beautifully preserved by laying the whole length of the cutting in a solution of glycerine and hot water. This method works particularly well with ivy fronds. If completely immersed in the solution ivy will absorb it through both leaves and stem.

Colourful ornamental gourds are easy to grow and popular with arrangers, but they need to be treated to retain their bright hues and a successful way of doing this is as follows:
- cut your well-matured gourd in half with a saw.
- scrape out all the pulp and seeds, ensuring the shell is perfectly clean.
- scrub the shell clean in soapy water.
- when clean, soak for five or six minutes in a mild solution of bleach – but do not rinse in fresh water.
- dry in shaded but airy place.
- once thoroughly dry you may glue the two halves together if you wish to use the gourd as a whole.

- finally, to bring out the colours to the full, wax outside of shell or spray with a light coat of varnish.

When arranging dry flowers and foliage you will find it useful to stabilize your container with sand, as the absence of water tends to make the vase of dry flowers top heavy and may cause it to topple over.

PLANTS TO DRY

Although it is possible to dry practically any flower, the following plants dry well and are extremely useful in arrangements:

The necks of zinnias are inclined to be weak and it is wise to insert a piece of florists wire through the flower into the stem to keep them firm, before hanging upside down for drying.

Achillea (yarrow) – pick open heads and hang dry for a fortnight.

Agapanthus – hang dry long-stemmed mature seed heads.

Centaurea (Dusty miller) – flower heads dry naturally.

Choisya ternata – dries beautifully by the glycerine method.

Crocosmia – flower seedheads dry naturally, while glycerine method is very successful for the leaves.

Elaeagnus pungens – dry the leaves by the glycerine method.

Eucalyptus cinerea (penny gum, florist's gum) – dry these blue-grey leaves by glycerine method.

Gypsophila – dries naturally in the vase or hung in bunches.

Limonium varieties (statice) – hang dry.

Lunaria (Honesty) – hang upside down when the seed is fully formed. To enjoy the silver discs it produces, gently rub off the outer casing.

Papaver varieties (poppy) – dry upright in a vase to retain attractive shapes.

Santolina – hang-dry the flowers.

Solidago canadensis (Golden rod) – hang dry, when fully opened and well shaped. Flowers turn a mellow gold shade.

Zinnias – these flowers dry well in silica gel, but to ensure the neck of flower does not bend, stick a piece of florist's wire through the head and into the stem to support it.

Nandina is best dried by the glycerine method.

XVI *The right equipment*

This selection of containers serves as a good start to the would be arranger, offering a variety of shapes for different work. Included are an epergnette flower holder which may be placed on top of a candlestick; a small statuette vase; a pedestal vase with ears; a variety of silver and copper containers; a small glass specimen vase; some clear glass vases of different shapes and a few small ceramic florist shop style bowls.

A wide deep cupboard has been put to excellent use as a floral workshop by one keen arranger, even the doors being used for bunches of dried grasses and flowers. The shelves contain useful arranging knick-knacks, from ribbons and string to a flower life extender, baskets, vases, gloves, knives, shells and even books on the subject of flower preparation.

Correct equipment is important with most sports, hobbies and pastimes and so too with flower arranging. Having the right props and tools adds greatly to the ease of operation and to your pleasure.

Containers and tools are the two major factors – the right vase or holder for a particular arrangement and the correct tool for a specific job. There is nothing worse than having only tall vases when in fact what you need is a flat bowl, or needing to cut wire mesh when you have only nail scissors with which to do the job. Ensure that you have a few of the basics – the luxury items can come later.

An old florist friend of mine in England was as enthusiastic a collector of fine vases as she was a flower arranger. She gathered containers of various kinds – baskets and boxes, pewter and porcelain, crystal and silver, even shells from around the world –

garnered from auctions and sales, tombola stalls and even junk heaps. Unfortunately her arrangements tended to set off her holders more than to complement the flowers.

In our household we tend to have a few favourites but it is very satisfying to have a choice and occasionally to use something totally different. This will overcome the temptation to stick to familiar designs – which, while easier, usually lack freshness and excitement. Using new material, both vase and flowers, forces you to apply your ingenuity and often to produce something exceptional.

For containers you can use practically anything, from picnic baskets and tea-pots to glorious samovars and spectacular crystal cylinders. Virtually any receptacle can be turned into a vase by lining it with glass jars or jam tins. With the advent of plastic it has

159

become possible to obtain cheap containers of all shapes and sizes, including milk powder buckets, baby baths and even disposable margarine tubs, all of which are suitable for lining interesting containers which would otherwise leak.

Most important, when selecting vases, choose containers to suit your home. Modern cylinders and squares look ghastly in Victorian-type settings, while ornate ceramics and fussy urns just do not fit in with contemporary interiors. Baskets are a good bet for most homes and suitable for all rooms from kitchens to bedrooms, whether displaying a few wild flowers or a bold arrangement for a banquet.

Silver, too, seems to fit in with most settings, as do copper and pewter, while a simple white bowl or vase sets off flowers without attracting too much attention to itself. Choose containers in colours which blend with your decor or in subdued shades to avoid clashing with your arrangements.

The following is a list of places where you are likely to need vases and suggestions of the most suitable containers:

• Low coffee tables need a rather low round bowl or floating bowl. Old-fashioned rose bowls are ideal.

• Dinner tables, depending on their shape, need medium low bowls either round for a round table or oblong or rectangular for an oval or long table.

• Mantlepieces require something either tall and narrow or with a flattish back to tuck in neatly against the wall.

• Windowsills demand something similar but on a smaller scale: a small dumpy vase, a jug or a wide cylinder or box-shaped – something that is not easily knocked down by a curtain billowing in a breeze or someone pulling a blind.

• Floors of halls, passageways or rooms need freestanding containers which are rather substantial and capable of holding a lot of water for tall-stemmed material such as bulrushes, strelitzias, branches of blossom or other bulky material. Walking-stick or umbrella stand pots are perfect for protea arrangements.

• Breakfast trays need tiny, dumpy vases that cannot be easily knocked over when the tray is carried.

• Shelves and room dividers can take a variety of shapes and sizes depending on the height of the shelves. Try an antique specimen vase or a tall cylinder or even a grouping of vases of different heights.

Among the containers useful for arranging are: old-fashioned rose bowls; baskets of various shapes; stemmed and footed vases; bottles, especially interesting ones such as wide, heavy-based wine bottles

Baskets are most useful containers for arranging flowers. With a bottle or plastic dish – even an empty margerine container – used as a holder, a few simple flowers can be made to look sensational.

and the blue glass chemist variety; clear glass or crystal cylinders and vases to display the attractive stems of flowers such as tulips and daffodils; candlecups (epergnettes), charming little flower-holders that fit on to candlesticks; floating-bowls; vases of various shapes, sizes and heights, even old tea-pots, egg cups, soup tureens and gravy boats.

When arranging, a rule of thumb with vases is that they should be one-third to two-fifths the height of the total arrangement, except when in high positions such as on mantlepieces or raised windowsills – what looks correct at eye-level is foreshortened when viewed from below. Trailing greenery is helpful in correcting perspective.

If you do a lot of flower arranging it is ideal to have an area set aside especially for all your containers and equipment, with a counter top on which you can work.

Rarely have I seen a better work area than that of a florist friend who at the back of his home has a wide double doored cupboard that opens out to reveal a work surface, backed by shelves which contain many of his holders and equipment. Beneath the counter-top are his buckets and baskets, while on the inside of the doors hang handy bunches of dried material. Adjoining the cupboard is a kitchen sink and a long open draining-board work surface. It is neat and compact and does not interfere with anyone or get in the way of kitchen staff.

Not everyone enjoys such luxury, but arrangers should aim at something approaching this, even if it is the unused servants quarters, a spare room or even just a cupboard in the kitchen to store your collection.

When it comes to equipment there are a number of essential items for gathering and arranging floral material. These include: a good pair of florist's scissors, the type with the nick at the bottom of one blade for cutting wire; a sharp knife; bird netting or mesh wire of some kind; pinholders of different shapes and sizes; floral foam, such as oasis; a bucket for gathering flowers and a small watering-can with a long pointed spout for filling and topping up vases and containers.

You will note the mention of a bucket for gathering flowers, rather than one of those

charming little flat baskets which, while they may look delightful in photographs, are not very practical. The reason for the bucket is that you can immediately plunge the stems of your cut flowers into water to keep them as fresh as possible.

Wire mesh, in spite of many modern aids such as plastic foam and pin cushions, remains the most popular material for supporting stems when arranging, but don't make the mistake of using mesh of too small a gauge. The 5 cm variety is by far the most useful and should be cut to about twice the height and twice the width of the container, crumpled, and secured in position with florist's tape.

There are a great variety of heavy-based pinholders available designed for containers of all shapes and sizes. There are even some known as well-pinholders, which come attached to their own cup for water.

Wire is always useful and no arranger should be without a reel of the pliable but fairly thick fuse variety. It has many uses including binding small bunches of flowers together and anchoring wire mesh to vases.

Green florist's wire is available from hardware stores, florists and even many garden centres and usually comes in 20 cm lengths, ideal for wiring individual flowers. This wire is stiff but pliable.

A sharp knife is most important both for cutting stems and for stripping leaves and is used by many arrangers in preference to secateurs.

If you plan to build up a good collection of useful accessories then there are many other worthwhile aids. In addition to those already mentioned are:

- Florist's plasticine
- Florist's tape
- Rose gatherers, including the long-handled variety for reaching into large bushes. These have a mechanism for cutting and holding the cut stem while you withdraw it from the bush.
- Rose strippers, for removing thorns.
- Dark green moss, for filling in baskets.
- Pipe cleaners.
- Ribbons of various colours.
- A small burner or cheap candle-holder and candle to burn the end of stems.
- A number of plastic buckets, the metal variety are rather burdensome for carrying around the garden.
- Clear glass marbles for supporting flowers in crystal vases.
- Some white stones for decoration and concealing pinholders.
- Glass tubes for holding orchids and for sticking into your wire mesh when you need

As with all hobbies the right tools make for fewer hassles and more pleasure in your pastime. They may be gathered as you progress but some extremely useful items are shown here: Chicken wire; a variety of pinholders; rose strippers and ribbons; oasis; an epergnette (upside down) for holding flowers on top of a candlestick; flower cutters, including a long-handled rose cutter which keeps you away from the thorns, by holding the rose for you while it cuts; a bunch of florist's wire and packet of crystals for extending the life of flowers.

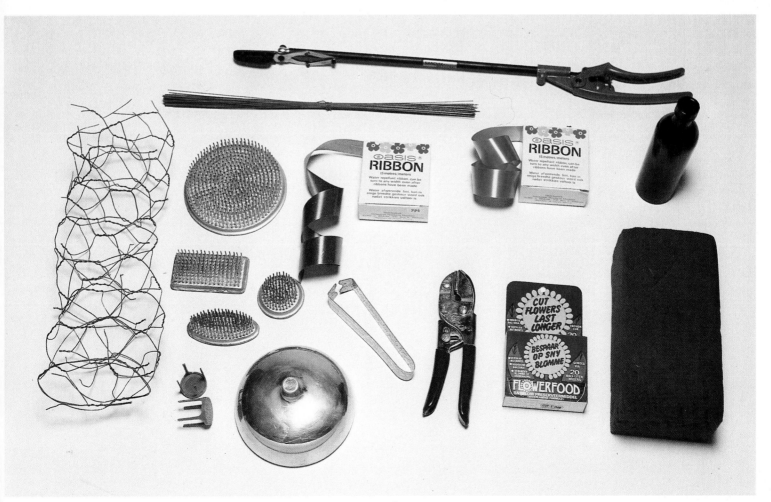

to increase the height of individual flowers in large arrangements.

- Driftwood for decoration.
- Hand sprays for misting flowers.
- Funnels for filling awkward arrangements with water.
- Glycerine. This is useful for preserving foliage material.
- Bases to protect furniture, such as bamboo or grass mats, rounds of polished wood or even cloths of various kinds.

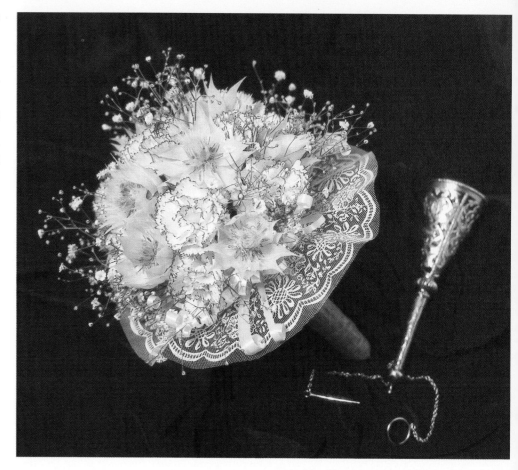

An unusual but useful piece of equipment worth having is this Victorian posy-holder.

Index

168